S0-AUS-914

DEVELOPING A SERVANT'S HEART

A 40 Day Devotional

Written by

The Staff of Central Christian Church

Henderson, NV

© 2004 Central Christian Church

Published by Central Christian Church
1001 New Beginnings Drive
Henderson, NV 89015
www.CentralChristian.com

ALL RIGHTS RESERVED.
No part of this publication may be reproduced, stored in a retrieval system, or transmitted in any form or by any means—for example, electronic, photocopy, recording—without the prior written permission of the publisher. The only exception is brief quotations in printed reviews.

Unless otherwise indicated, Scripture quotations are taken from the HOLY BIBLE, NEW INTERNATIONAL VERSION®. NIV®. Copyright © 1973, 1978, 1984 by International Bible Society. Used by permission of Zondervan. All rights reserved.

Scripture quotations marked (CEV) are taken from the Contemporary English Version. Copyright © 1991, 1992, 1995 by American Bible Society. Used by permission.

Scripture quotations marked (GNT) are taken from the Good News Translation - Second Edition © 1992 by American Bible Society. Used by permission.

Scripture marked KJV is taken from the HOLY BIBLE, King James Version

Scripture quotations marked TLB are taken from The Living Bible, Copyright © 1971. Used by permission of Tyndale House Publishers, Inc., Wheaton, Illinois 60189. All rights reserved.

Scripture marked MSG is taken from *The Message*, by Eugene H. Peterson, Copyright © 1993, 1994, 1995, 1996, 2000, 2001, 2002. Used by permission of NavPress Publishing Group. All rights reserved.

Scripture marked NASB is taken from the New American Standard Bible®, Copyright © 1960, 1962, 1963, 1968, 1971, 1972, 1973, 1975, 1977, 1995 by The Lockman Foundation. Used by permission.

Scripture quotations marked "NCV" are taken from the New Century Version®. Copyright © 1987, 1988, 1991 by Word Publishing, a division of Thomas Nelson. Used by permission. All rights reserved.

Scripture quotations marked "NKJV" are taken from the New King James Version. Copyright © 1982 by Thomas Nelson, Inc. Used by permission. All rights reserved.

Scripture quotations marked (NLT) are taken from the Holy Bible, New Living Translation, Copyright © 1996. Used by permission of Tyndale House Publishers, Inc., Wheaton, Illinois 60189. All rights reserved.

ISBN 1-888741-26-0

Cover design and book layout by PlainJoe Studios

Printed in the United States of America

10 9 8 7 6 5 4 3 2 1

TABLE OF CONTENTS

INTRODUCTION

Welcome to the 40-day adventure of exploring your God-given purpose! As you read this book, you will learn more about developing the kind of servant's heart that God designed for you. You'll also discover the joy and fulfillment of using your unique wiring and gifting to make a difference in this world for God. If you prayerfully reflect on the principles found on these pages and apply them in your life, you will discover the kind of abundant life Jesus was talking about when He said He had come that we may have life and have it to the fullest extent (John 10:10 NIV).

This book was originally conceived and designed to be a handbook for the 40-Day Developing a Servant's Heart campaign at Central Christian Church in Henderson, Nevada. It was written by twenty-six members of the Central Christian Church staff who each brought their unique personalities and perspectives to the topic of servant-hood. The book itself is modeled after Rick Warren's book, *The Purpose Driven Life,* and the 40 Days of Purpose Campaign originally developed by Saddleback Community Church in Lake Forest, California. If you have not yet read

The Purpose Driven Life, I recommend you read it as a follow-up to this book. God is using it to change the hearts of millions around the world.

To get the most from this book, I strongly urge you to only read one chapter a day. Spend some time considering the *Point to Ponder* and *Questions to Consider* at the end of each chapter. Look up the Biblical passages referenced by the authors and prayerfully consider how you might better fulfill your God-given purpose. Make an appointment to read one chapter each day and set aside a few minutes to reflect on what you read. By making this reading a priority for the next 40 days, you'll begin to experience a shift in your attitude and perspective and discover more about God's unique purpose for your life. Enjoy the journey!

Jud Wilhite
Senior Pastor, Central Christian Church
Henderson, NV

ACKNOWLEDGEMENTS

This project would not be possible without the contributions of the staff of Central Christian Church, Henderson, Nevada who prayerfully, creatively and powerfully communicated God's truth through their written words. They have modeled the kind of servant's heart this book discusses both in the development of this book and in their daily ministries. God continues to use their faithful service to transform the lives of people in Southern Nevada and around the world.

We would also like to thank our friends at PlainJoe Studios in Corona, California. Without their help this project would not have been possible. Through their relationship with God they guided us to a finished product that continues to have Spirit-led impact in the lives it touches. To Him and PlainJoe we are grateful.

WEEK 1

RECOGNIZING YOUR DESIGN

"I praise you because I am fearfully and wonderfully made; your works are wonderful, I know that full well."

Psalm 139:14 (NIV)

DAY 1

EARLY MORNING SURPRISE

The moments in between the laughter and the talking, in between the struggles and the tears, in between the triumphs and the losses—these are the moments that speak to us. When we cry out, "There must be more to life than this!" It is during these contemplative moments that God reaches out and speaks to us. He invites us to live a life of purposeful

"For we are God's workmanship, created in Christ Jesus to do good works, which God prepared in advance for us to do."

Ephesians 2:10 (NIV)

service. A life outside of our own world views and free of the monotony of day-to-day living. God did not create us to blindly pursue our own ambitions. He created each of us with a divine purpose and it is only

when we submit to His will and plan for our lives that we truly live the life we were created for. To live a life fulfilled we must realize that it's not about us because it's all about Him.

It was 2 a.m. on a cold, rainy night seven years ago—just two days before Thanksgiving. As a restaurant manager, I was elbow deep in cranberry sauce for the upcoming turkey feast when suddenly, my wife popped in. With tears streaming down her troubled face, her words were brief and to the point, "We have to talk." A million thoughts raced through my mind but I quickly rested on a single one. As we stepped outside

"When your focus changes from yourself to God, you begin to evolve as God's masterpiece."

I simply said, "You're pregnant." A quiet nod confirmed my thoughts and fears.

Just three weeks prior to this unexpected news, we had packed up the car and said our farewells to everyone we knew and loved in California. We were beginning a new life in Las Vegas. So the questions that night came in stereo rapid fire. How are we going to afford a baby? How will we take care of a baby? How will this affect our plans? Our dreams? Our goals? All we could think of were material needs for the baby and ourselves; we wondered how our lives would change from that moment on.

Nine months later our first child, a baby boy, entered this world. The questions from that rainy night were still fresh in our minds. But by making some adjustments and sacrifices, we managed our newfound responsibilities; providing and caring for our son took top priority. As parents we see this as our duty, our job if you will, to ensure that our child has everything he needs; and as believers we know it's God's plan for us as well.

God's plan, however, goes much deeper, beyond providing for our physical needs. Ephesians 2:10 (NIV) says, "For we are God's workmanship, created in Christ Jesus to do good works, which God prepared in advance for us to do." We are made in the image of God. The Bible tells us in Genesis 1:27 (NIV), "God created man in his own image in the image of God he created him; male and female he created them." While human limitations sometimes prevent us from fulfilling our "good deeds," we can break through them by our faith in Christ. In caring for my children, I'm not only fulfilling my duties as a father, but also glorifying God by living out His purpose for me.

Do you feel unsure of God's purpose for you or the "good works" you should do? The "good works" in Ephesians 2:10 are simply the deeds you do in daily life through your job, your responsibilities at home, your friendships, your ministry at church, or any other role you live out. God intentionally put you in each of these roles to give you opportunities to glorify Him. "Good works" are those tasks beneficial to others that He prepared in advance for you to do. The "do" part is more physical in nature, and calls you to get up and go! But go where? And do what? The Bible says, "I glorify you on earth by completing down to the last detail what you assigned me to do" (John 17:4, MSG). Simply put, always look for opportunities to serve others and bring glory to God.

So the question, "Why on earth am I here?" is answered in the

WEEK ONE

routine of your everyday life. You must now ask yourself, "Do I live for God's purpose or my own?" It is by the grace of God and your faith in Christ that you are saved. Ephesians 2:8-9 (NIV) says, "For it is by grace you have been saved, through faith—and this is not from yourselves, it is the gift of God—not by works, so that no one can boast." Keeping this humble attitude will help you "do the good works" and be the masterpiece God created you to be. While the task or act itself is physical, your attitude should be purely spiritual. When your focus changes from yourself to God, you begin to evolve as God's masterpiece. When your lifestyle becomes dependent on Him, you begin to realize your purpose for being here on earth.

Thinking back to that rainy night, I now realize that the worries we had were natural but selfish in and of themselves. Today, as I live my life as a father, I glorify God in doing so, as this is His purpose for me. With this mindset, any "good works" I perform are an act of worship to Him, and not about my own selfish needs, dreams and goals. So do I feel confident that I'm fulfilling God's purpose as a father to my son? One day, my wife mistakenly arrived very late in picking up our now six-year-old son after school. She fully expected to find a very scared and tearful little boy. Surprisingly, he appeared calm and patient. On the way home, a very apologetic mommy asked if he was okay, only to hear him confidently respond, "It's okay Mommy, God was with me." I guess we're well on our way. Glory be to God.

POINT TO PONDER

There's a greater reason for everything you do.

VERSE TO REMEMBER

"For we are God's workmanship, created in Christ Jesus to do good works, which God prepared in advance for us to do."

Ephesians 2:10 (NIV)

QUESTION TO CONSIDER

Are you living for God's purpose or your own?

WEEK ONE

DAY 1

NOTES

MORE
THAN
A SONG

You were created to worship! God chose to create you for His pleasure and enjoyment. Psalm 139:13-14 (NIV) says, "For you created my inmost being; you knit me together in my mother's womb. I praise you because I am fearfully and wonderfully made; your works are wonderful, I know that full well." Isn't it amazing that God specifically and

> *"So love the Lord God with all your passion and prayer and intelligence and energy."*
>
> Mark 12:30 (MSG)

uniquely designed you for His pleasure and enjoyment? You were not a mistake! You were created for a purpose and that purpose was to worship Him. When we begin to grasp this incredible fact, it can revolution-

WEEK ONE

ize our understanding of what true worship is all about. It's all about God! Everything that we do and say becomes an act of worship to Him.

Worship manifests itself in many unique ways. Have you ever noticed how people respond at a concert or sporting event? They stand with their hands in the air, raise their voices, cheer or give accolades to their favorite team or recording artist. It's in our nature to worship—we do it every day! The question is how, what or whom will you worship? Author Louie Giglio gives a definition of worship in his book, *The Air I Breathe*, "Worship is our response to what we value most." What is it that you value most in life? Whatever it is, you're likely responding to it in worship.

For many, worship is just a synonym for songs sung in church before a pastor teaches. In fact, every part of a worship service is an act of worship: singing, praying, Scripture reading, meditating, partaking in Communion, celebrating new life through baptism, engaging in the teacher's message and even greeting those around you.

Worship also reaches far beyond what takes place in church. It's not just a *part* of your life—it *is* your life! The Bible says, "Give thanks to the Lord, proclaim his greatness; tell the nations what he has done. Sing praise to the Lord; tell the wonderful things he has done. Be glad that we belong to him; let all who worship him rejoice! Go to the Lord for help, and **worship him continually**" (1 Chronicles 16:8-11, GN).

God gave you a unique personality that impacts the way you live your life and how you connect with God in worship. In his book, *Sacred Pathways*, author Gary Thomas presents nine spiritual temperaments or pathways of worship.

- *Naturalists* feel closest to God when they are out-of-doors in a natural setting.
- *Sensates* worship God in ways using their senses of sight, sound, taste, smell and touch.
- *Traditionalists* are drawn toward ritual and symbol.
- *Ascetics* prefer to experience God in solitude and simplicity.
- *Activists* feel that they worship God by contributing toward justice and the enhancement of life in the world.
- *Caregivers* simply love God by loving others.
- *Enthusiasts* worship God through mystery and celebration.
- *Contemplatives* simply worship God through contemplation.
- *Intellectuals* love God with their minds by seeking foundational Biblical truth.

Which of these pathways best resonates with your personality? Gaining an understanding of the unique way God created you helps broaden and expand your understanding of how you most naturally experience God in worship.

God gave you emotions and feelings to help you experience and enjoy life to the fullest. These emotions play a vital role in your daily life. If you're a parent, you've experienced joy when your child does something to make you proud or when they wrap their arms around you and tell you how much they love you. Nothing pleases a parent more! Remember when you were a child and did things to try to please your parents? Maybe it was trying to hit a home run, dancing at a recital or going beyond the call of duty in helping with the household chores.

WEEK ONE

We all have that inborn desire to please our parents and gain their love and acceptance. As a child of God, you don't have to try to gain His acceptance. He is proud of you and loves you unconditionally. So go ahead, run into His gracious, loving arms. Intimately and emotionally express your love to your Heavenly Father.

One of the most important steps toward developing a servant's heart is to fully surrender every part of your life to God and to live every aspect of your life as an act of worship to Him. Embrace the awesome challenge that lies in this verse,

"Worship is our response to what we value most."

Louie Giglio

"Love the Lord your God with all your heart and with all your soul and with all your mind and with all your strength" (Mark 12:30, NIV). Right now, ask God to help you fully realize why He created you. Ask Him to help you live out this truth in the way you handle your business affairs, love your spouse, care for your family, share your faith, serve others or how you express your heart in worship to a God who loves you and uniquely created you for His pleasure. Remember, it's not about you; it's all about Him!

POINT TO PONDER

You were created to worship.

VERSE TO REMEMBER

"Love the Lord your God with all your heart and with all your soul and with all your mind and with all your strength." Mark 12:30 (NIV)

QUESTION TO CONSIDER

How can you learn to fully grasp the fact that God uniquely designed you to worship Him with every part of your life?

Louie Giglio; from his book, *The Air I Breathe* (Copyright 2003 by Louie Giglio/Published by Multnoma Publishers)

WEEK ONE

DAY 2

D A Y 3

MICHAEL'S SONG

God wants a family and He created you to be part of it. The entire Bible is a story of God building a family who will love, honor and reign with Him forever. When we place our faith in Christ, God becomes our Father, we become His children, other believers become our brothers and sisters and the church becomes our spiritual family.

"So in Christ we who are many form one body, and each member belongs to all the others."

Romans 12:5 (NIV)

Ephesians 2:19b (LB) says, "You are members of God's very own family, citizens of God's country, and you belong in God's household with every other Christian." Think about that. If you're a believer, you're

a member of God's family. You get the family name and all the family privileges. Being part of God's family is the greatest privilege we could ever have.

The family of God includes all believers past, present and future. In Romans 12:5 Paul says, "Each member belongs to the other." To Paul the word "member" meant being a vital organ of a living body; an indispensable, interconnected part of the Body of Christ. An organ cannot exist on its own and neither can you. Every believer in Christ needs a place to belong, and a loving community to be a part of. But many believers have never experienced true community. They only know people on a superficial level.

"How's it going at work, Jack?"

"Fine, Mike. Hey, I see you got new tires on your truck."

"Got 'em on sale. Do you have a busy week?"

"Not too bad, same ol' same ol'."

"Great fellowshipping with you, Jack."

"Same here, Mike."

And that's about it! But the Bible says true fellowship goes well below the surface.

Masks come off, conversations get deep, hearts get vulnerable, lives are shared, accountability is invited and tenderness flows. People really do become like brothers and sisters.

A few years ago a story appeared in *Women's Day* magazine. It told of a three-year-old boy who would sing to his unborn sister. Day after day, night after night, Michael sang to his sister in Mommy's tummy. The pregnancy progressed normally for Karen, but complications arose

during delivery. After hours of labor Michael's little sister was finally born, but her condition was serious. With sirens howling in the night, the infant is rushed to the neonatal intensive care unit at a hospital in nearby Knoxville.

The days inched by. The little girl got worse. The pediatric specialist told the parents, "There's very little hope. Be prepared for the worst."

Karen and her husband contacted a local cemetery about a burial plot. They'd prepared a special room in their home for the new baby; now they had to plan a funeral. Children aren't allowed in intensive care, but Michael kept begging his parents to let him see his sister. "I want to sing to her," he says.

Week two arrives in intensive care. It looks as if a funeral will

> "They'd prepared a special room in their home for the new baby; now they had to plan a funeral."

come before the week is over. Michael keeps pleading to sing to his sister, so Karen made up her mind. She would take Michael whether they liked it or not. If he didn't see his sister then, he might never see her alive. She dressed him in oversized scrubs and marched him into the ICU. He looked like a walking laundry basket but the head nurse recognized him as a child and bellowed; "Get that kid out of here now! No children are allowed in ICU."

The mother in Karen rose up strong. Her usual mild-mannered nature transformed as she glared steel-eyed into the head nurse's face,

WEEK ONE

her lips a firm line. "He is not leaving until he sings to his sister!" Karen towed Michael to his sister's bedside. He gazed at the tiny infant losing her battle to live. And he began to sing. In the pure-hearted voice of a three-year-old, Michael sang: "You are my sunshine, my only sunshine, you make me happy when skies are gray..." Instantly the baby girl responded. The pulse rate became calm and steady. Michael kept on singing. "You'll never know, dear, how much I love you, Please don't take my sunshine away..."

The ragged, strained breathing became as smooth as a kitten's purr. Michael kept on singing. "The other night, dear, as I lay sleeping, I dreamed I held you in my arms..." Michael's little sister relaxed, as rest, healing rest, seemed to sweep over her. Michael kept on singing. Tears conquered the face of the bossy head nurse. Karen glowed. "You are my sunshine, my only sunshine. Please don't, take my sunshine away."

Funeral plans were scrapped. The next day, the very next day, the little girl is well enough to go home! *Woman's Day* magazine called it "The Miracle of a Brother's Song." The medical staff just called it a miracle. Karen called it a miracle of God's love.

Biblical community is being committed to each other and to Jesus Christ just as little Michael was to his newborn sister. Biblical community is where believers experience life on a heart-to-heart, soul-to-soul level; where believers gather together to share their hearts on the deepest levels; where people compassionately walk with each other through life's problems and pain; where everyone feels empowered to make a difference through his or her spiritual gifts; where prayer, worship and the Word of God is taught and lived out; where those who have financial

gain give to those who are in need and where people who have friends and family far from God do whatever it takes to reach them with the Gospel. This is where the miracle of new life and heart transformation takes place. Now don't you want to be a part of that kind of family?

POINT TO PONDER

You were formed for God's family.

VERSE TO REMEMBER

"So in Christ we who are many form one body, and each member belongs to all the others." Romans 12:5 (NIV)

QUESTIONS TO CONSIDER

What is one thing you can do to connect with another believer to experience life together this week? On a regular basis?

WEEK ONE

DAY 3

NOTES

EYE
ON THE
GOAL

An artist envisions a picture before painting it. A musician hears a song in his thoughts before writing it. God knew the end result when He created you. He had a clear vision of who He wanted you to be before you were born. And do you know what He pictured? He pictured Jesus. That's because God created you to be like His Son, Jesus Christ. The Bible

"God knew what he was doing from the very beginning. He decided from the outset to shape the lives of those who love him along the same lines as the life of his Son. The Son stands first in the line of humanity he restored. We see the original and intended shape of our lives there in him."

Romans 8:29 (MSG)

WEEK ONE

says, "God knew what he was doing from the very beginning. He decided from the outset to shape the lives of those who love him along the same lines as the life of his Son. The Son stands first in the line of humanity he restored. We see the original and intended shape of our lives there in him" (Romans 8:29, MSG). God's innovative design for your life is for you to grow, change and transform to become like his Son, Jesus. Philippians 2:5 (NIV) says, "Your attitude should be the same as that of Christ Jesus."

When you came to believe in Jesus, did you assume you'd done all you were supposed to do? Did you feel like you crossed the finish line? Did you think you could now sit tight and wait for heaven? It's true that Jesus gave His life so you could join Him in heaven. But God has plans for you on earth first. Believing in Jesus and being baptized in His name is not the final destination; it's the starting line! It's the beginning of an exciting race. Following Christ is a life-long adventurous journey leading to dramatic changes in your life on earth and culminating in an eternal relationship with God in heaven.

> "God knew the end result when He created you. He had a clear vision of who He wanted you to be before you were born."

An athlete doesn't work hard just to make the team. He wants to compete at the highest level attainable and win. Can you imagine an athlete whose end goal is making the Olympic team? What if he decides not to compete because his dream was just to make the team? He's thrilled to get the coveted USA warm-ups and wave to his family and friends during Opening Ceremonies. Now wouldn't you think he was crazy? Wouldn't you think he let down his teammates and missed out on an even greater experience by not competing? Wouldn't you think he aimed short of the ultimate goal?

As a believer in Jesus Christ your end goal is to become more and more like Him. Paul talks about this goal and his single-minded determination to reach it. He writes, "I want to know Christ and the power of his resurrection and the fellowship of his sufferings… Not that I have already obtained all this or have already been made perfect, but I press on to take hold of that for which Christ Jesus took hold of me. Brothers, I do not consider myself yet to have taken hold of it. But one thing I do: Forgetting what is behind and straining toward what is ahead, I press on toward the goal to win the prize for which God has called me heavenward in Christ Jesus" (Philippians 3:10-14, NIV).

Paul understood his goal and the direction of his life. The desire to know Jesus and follow Him closely should also be your goal as a Christian. In the very next verse Paul encourages, "So let's keep focused on that goal, those of us who want everything God has for us. If any of you have something else in mind, something less than total commitment, God will clear your blurred vision—you'll see it yet" (Philippians 3:15, MSG).

So what should this change look like in your life? As you become more like Christ, how will you be different?

1. You'll naturally want to tell others about Christ's love and how His grace is transforming you.

2. You'll want to serve others with your time, talent and treasures.

3. You'll continue growing in your relationship with God by practicing spiritual disciplines and acquiring biblical knowledge.

4. You'll live your life in authentic biblical community.

5. You'll respond to God's love by pursuing a lifestyle of worship.

6. You'll better understand who Christ made you to be and make every effort to reach the world by living out the mission of the church.

When you're growing like Christ you'll begin experiencing these changes. It's not always easy. It requires effort, diligence and training. You don't become a world-class athlete by impulsively deciding to compete in the Olympic trials. You only reach this level through years of perseverance and keeping your eye on the goal. There's a huge difference between short-term *trying* and long-term *training*. 1 Timothy 4:7 (NIV) says, "Train yourself to be godly." This is a life-long process. Coming to faith is not an end. It's a wonderful beginning leading to an exciting lifetime adventure.

POINT TO PONDER

God created you to be like His Son, Jesus Christ.

VERSE TO REMEMBER

"God knew what he was doing from the very beginning. He decided from the outset to shape the lives of those who love him along the same lines as the life of his Son. The Son stands first in the line of humanity he restored. We see the original and intended shape of our lives there in him." Romans 8:29 (MSG)

QUESTIONS TO CONSIDER

When you look at the list of six characteristics of a changed life, how are you doing in these areas? What tangible and specific things can you do to grow in one or two of these areas?

WEEK ONE

NOTES

DAY 5

TAKING
THE
STAGE

Two thousand years ago, Jesus began His mission saying, "The kingdom of God is near. Repent and believe the good news!" (Mark 1:15, NIV). He envisioned a new kingdom, a new way of living with new purposes

"Be wise in the way you act toward outsiders; make the most of every opportunity."

Colossians 4:5 (NIV)

and values. Jesus lived, taught and gave His life on a cross to see God's vision of this new reality brought to light. In Revelation, John records:

> After these things I looked, and behold, a great multitude which no one could count, from every nation and all tribes and peoples and

WEEK ONE

37

tongues, standing before the throne and before the Lamb, clothed in white robes, and palm branches were in their hands; and they cry out with a loud voice, saying, "Salvation to our God who sits on the throne, and to the Lamb." (Revelation 7:9-10, NASB)

God is the writer, producer and casting director of this drama. He's ready for you to take the stage. No audition or experience required. As God's masterpiece you are blessed to be a blessing to people near and far. As a Christ-follower it's your privilege to **know Him and make Him known**.

Eric Liddell took the stage for Christ. He was a Scotsman who competed in the Olympic 100-meter dash held in Paris in 1924. The movie, *Chariots of Fire*, depicts his life. Following the Olympics, Liddell lived in China as a missionary. His words express today's devotion. "We are all missionaries...wherever we go, we either bring people nearer to Christ, or we repel them from Christ."

Do you see your life this way? Do you see yourself as a missionary drawing people nearer to Christ or driving them further from Him? Of course the word missionary has a specific definition, but every follower of Jesus is His representative. Paul said, "We are therefore Christ's ambassadors, as though God were making His appeal through us" (2 Corinthians 5:20a, NIV). Every Christ-follower is His ambassador on earth. It's our privilege to make Him known in our neighborhoods and even to the nations.

Paul gives sound advice on the "how" part of the mission. He wrote to the believers in Colossae these words, "Be wise in the way you act

toward outsiders; make the most of every opportunity. Let your conversation be always full of grace, seasoned with salt, so that you may know
how to answer everyone" (Colossians 4:5-6, NIV). Realize who you are.
You represent Jesus in all you do and say. Let's look at this passage a
little closer.

The first step in evangelism that Paul addresses is the way we live.
Every day you live with and
encounter people who are not
Christ-followers. How do they
perceive you? Your behavior
gives credibility to what you
say. You were called to live
without excuses so those on the
outside can claim no excuses
due to your conduct. What kind
of ambassador are you? Are
you imitating Jesus? Are you
attracting others to Him by liv-

"We are all missionaries
. . . wherever we go,
we either bring people
nearer to Christ, or we
repel them from Christ."

Eric Liddell, Olympian and
Missionary to China

ing as He called you to? Are you displaying His wisdom in all you do?
Moses prayed, "Teach us to number our days aright, that we may gain a
heart of wisdom" (Psalm 90:12, NIV). When our actions line up with our
words we make the most of every opportunity.

Secondly, Paul addresses our speech. A consistent life must be consistent in speech. Time is short. Regard every interaction, conversation and
encounter with someone outside Christ as an opportunity. Paul advises
that we redeem the time, buy it up, ransom it back and make the most of

WEEK ONE

every opportunity. Be ready and know how to respond to every person. It takes discipline and training but Paul's two-pronged approach says to temper your words with grace and season your words with salt.

1. **Temper your words with grace.** Make a point to use words and a manner of speech that are useful, helpful, kind and appropriate for the moment. Whether in the break room, at lunch, in the office, at school or at home, "Do not let any unwholesome talk come out of your mouths, but only what is helpful for building others up according to their needs, that it may benefit those who listen" (Ephesians 4:29, NIV). Gracious speech marks who we are. Gracious speech energizes our witness.

2. **Season your words with salt.** Gracious speech must be effectively seasoned, carefully chosen words full of flavor—nothing dull or trite. Imagine your speech today as a savoring influence on everyone you encounter; choose words that hold sustaining influence, and preserve all that you believe. Jesus said, "You are the salt of the earth. But if the salt loses its saltiness, how can it be made salty again? It is no longer good for anything, except to be thrown out and trampled by men" (Matthew 5:13, NIV). Winsome words are thoughtful, clearly communicated and properly seasoned.

Are you ready to be part of the drama and take the stage for Christ? Time is short. There's no room for stage fright or shallow excuses. As His ambassador, you're commissioned for God's mission of making Jesus known in your sphere of influence, so "Be wise in the way you act toward outsiders; make the most of every opportunity" (Colossians 4:5, NIV).

POINT TO PONDER
You are Christ's ambassador in your sphere of influence.

VERSE TO REMEMBER
"Be wise in the way you act toward outsiders; make the most of every opportunity." Colossians 4:5 (NIV)

QUESTION TO CONSIDER
Are you bringing people nearer to Christ through your words and actions or sending them further away?

WEEK ONE

D A Y 5

NOTES

GREAT PLANS, FREE GIFTS.

God has great plans for you. They're distinct, exciting and unique to you. He's even specifically wired you to accomplish those plans. But make no mistake about it; these are not plans for someday down the road in the distant future. They're not for when you get older, after you graduate, or when the kids are grown. No, God has great plans for you *right now*.

"Each one should use whatever gift he has received to serve others, faithfully administering God's grace in its various forms."

1 Peter 4:10 (NIV)

WEEK ONE

Once you accept Jesus Christ as your Lord and Savior and invite Him into your life, you're on an amazing journey. Part of that journey includes discovering the gifts He gave you. In 1 Corinthians 12:1 (NIV) Paul says, "Now about spiritual gifts, I do not want you to be ignorant." Spiritual gifts are the tools needed to build the church. They help you do ministry and enable you to grow more like Christ.

More specifically, spiritual gifts are special abilities the Holy Spirit gives to each new believer at conversion. They're a precious expression of God's love for us. Your spiritual gifts enable you to minister to others and build up the body of Christ. You don't deserve them, you can't earn them—they're free and they're truly amazing. Few things in life offer more fulfillment than the thrill of discovering and using your unique gifts.

"God has great plans for you *right now.*"

1 Peter 4:10 (NIV) says, "Each one should use whatever gift he has received to serve others, faithfully administering God's grace in its various forms." You may not think you have any special gifts or talents, but Peter says "each one," and that means you! He even goes a step further, telling us to find out what our gift is and to use it faithfully. God didn't give us these gifts to hoard selfishly. One day He wants to tell us, "Well done good and faithful servant..." (Matthew 25:23, NIV).

God also gave you a one-of-a-kind personality, talents, treasures and passions. He's given you different experiences than anyone else and your own unique perspective on those experiences. All of these things come together to shape you. It's what makes you uniquely you. Now you have the joy of deciding what to do about it. What will you do with your distinct blend of gifts, talents, experiences and personality?

Consider Christ's example. In Mark 10:45 (NIV) Jesus says, "For even the Son of Man did not come to be served, but to serve, and to give his life as a ransom for many." Then in John 12:26 (NIV) He says, "Whoever serves me must follow me; and where I am, my servant also will be. My Father will honor the one who serves me." Jesus is saying, don't ask what others can do for you. Ask what you can do to serve God and others. How can you give back? How can you use your gifts? Where can you make a difference in advancing God's kingdom?

It flies in the face of society's selfish tendencies, doesn't it? But this life is not about you or me. We serve God best by serving others. Status, power and prestige quickly fade. But spending time with a child, building relationships with people who need to know Christ, sharing an encouraging Bible verse with a hurting friend—those are kingdom-building projects. You can make a difference. No act of service for God is too small. In Matthew 10:42 (NIV) Jesus says, "If anyone gives even a cup of cold water to one of these little ones because he is my disciple, I tell you the truth, he will certainly not lose his reward."

Are you open to the plans He has for you? Are you making yourself available? Or are you so wrapped up in your own agenda that you're missing out on His amazing plan for you? He only asks that we love Him and are faithful. It's so simple! True servants willingly perform less than glamorous tasks. True servants step up when needed, even when it's inconvenient. True servants faithfully serve with their whole heart, know-

WEEK ONE

ing it's the Lord they are serving and not man. God's grace is more than sufficient to supply all our needs. Pray that His will be done through you, by the way he uniquely gifted you. Let His grace flow through you as you discover the joy of serving Him and others by using your amazing gifts.

"Therefore, my dear brothers, stand firm. Let nothing move you. Always give yourselves fully to the work of the Lord, because you know that your labor in the Lord is not in vain" (1 Corinthians 15:58, NIV).

POINT TO PONDER

Few things in life offer more fulfillment than the thrill of discovering and using your unique gifts.

VERSE TO REMEMBER

"Whoever wants to be great must become a servant." Mark 10:43b (MSG)

QUESTIONS TO CONSIDER

Are you currently serving God? Are you open and available to His call for you life?

NOTES

A
LIFE
WELL-LIVED

No matter how full and successful your life, you're not truly living until you're living out God's purposes in your life. This week we've briefly looked at those purposes. We've learned we're not on this earth by accident. God put us here for a reason. The ultimate pursuit of our lives is to discover and fulfill those purposes. We learned that God's purposes

> *"For to me, to live is Christ,*
> *and to die is gain."*
> Philippians 1:21 (NIV)

include bringing Him pleasure through worship, experiencing godly relationships through community, growing more like Jesus through discipleship, sharing the good news of new life in Christ through our life-mission and using our gifts to honor God through serving.

During this devotional series we're taking a closer look at God's purpose of servant-hood in our lives. We'll examine the servant life of Jesus and learn how to discover and use our unique design and gifts for God. Once we understand God's purpose in our lives, we can experience what Jesus had in mind when He said, "I came so they can have real and eternal life, more and better life than they ever dreamed of" (John 10:10, MSG). Diane Holladay discovered this "more and better life" at a very personal level last year when she completed the 40 *Days of Purpose* Bible study.

Diane had lived a life filled with excitement and adventure. She'd worked at the biggest Las Vegas hotels as a dancer and shared the stage with some of the greatest names of her generation. She knew Frank Sinatra, Nat King Cole, Ella Fitzgerald and anyone who was anyone in the Las Vegas entertainment scene.

Through it all, Jesus was always a part of her life. She was a member of her church for many years before joining the staff as an administrative assistant five years ago. When she learned her congregation was going to study *The 40 Days of Purpose* collectively as a church last year, she was thrilled. Diane had already read most of Rick Warren's book, *The Purpose Driven Life**, around which the *40-Days of Purpose* experience was built. But she was eager to discover more about her God-given purpose.

Shortly before diving into the *40Days of Purpose* experience, Diane received disheartening news. She had a serious blood disorder. Treatments could help control the disease but chemotherapy was her only hope for a cure. As the disease progressed she grew weaker and weaker. Still, she continued to work, hiding her illness and fatigue as best she could.

WEEK ONE

During this time, she made her *40Days of Purpose* group a priority, faithfully reading each day's devotional and discussing it with her small group. Together they learned and shared new depths of understanding and purpose in their relationships with Jesus. Diane came to understand God's love and purpose for her life in a whole new way. She fully trusted that whether or not her health returned, God would always be there for her. What had long been a strong faith grew yet stronger and blossomed into a new peace and assurance she'd never known before. That peace would soon be put to the test.

By the end of the *40Days of Purpose* experience, Diane's condition had grown worse. Her doctors realized they had to take serious action to try to save her life. The regular injections intended to restore her slipping blood cell counts had proven insufficient. Diane's doctors recommended chemotherapy to wipe out the disease. The risk was significant. Her body was already so weakened that chemotherapy could worsen her condition and possibly even lead to her death. But it was the last medical hope for a cure.

As Diane lay in the hospital processing this weighty decision, she called her church and asked to have a pastor meet and talk with her. They met alone and prayed together, wrestling through her decision. With no better option, she chose to fight the disease by undergoing chemotherapy. She fully understood the damage that could result from the treatment, but she also had peace. No matter what happened, God would be with her and fulfill His purposes for her life. Describing the peace she felt, she quoted Paul from Philippians 1:21 (NIV), "For to me, to live is Christ, and to die is gain." Diane would face treatment without fear, knowing she would either continue living out her God-given purpose in *this* life or in the life to come. Just as it says in Romans 8:38-39, even death would not separate her from the love of God that is in Jesus.

The chemotherapy was too much for her weak body. Diane went home to Jesus a few days after receiving treatment. Even in their grief, friends and loved ones were inspired by Diane's life and faith to the end. Hundreds of people came to her funeral to pay tribute to her memory. Tears were shed, the loss was great, but it was also a celebration of a life well lived in Christ and a subsequent homecoming. As if she herself was there directing, Diane's funeral became a tribute to Jesus Christ. Because, with all the excitement, glamour and adventure of her life, in the end what truly mattered was Diane's relationship with Christ and her commitment to live out God's purposes, in life and even in death.

"What had long been a strong faith grew yet stronger and blossomed into a new peace and assurance she'd never known before."

Diane came to understand God's purposes for her life in a deep and personal way through her *40Days of Purpose* experience last year. It strengthened her faith and carried her through a difficult time she never expected. It's my prayer that as you venture through this devotional experience you too will come to understand God's purposes for your life in a new and profound way. May your faith grow so deep and strong you'll be ready to endure whatever challenges lie ahead in your life.

WEEK ONE

POINT TO PONDER

True living is discovering and fulfilling your God-given purpose.

VERSE TO REMEMBER

"For to me, to live is Christ, and to die is gain." Philippians 1:21 (NIV)

QUESTIONS TO CONSIDER

Do you know God's purposes for your life? If so, are you living them out? If not, what will you do to discover them?

*Rick Warren, *The Purpose Driven Life*
(Grand Rapids, MI: Zondervan, 2002)

NOTES

W E E K   2

DEVELOPING YOUR HEART

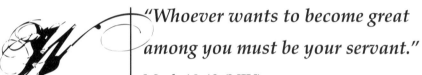

"Whoever wants to become great among you must be your servant."

Mark 19:43 (NIV)

THE
CHOICE

"Your attitude should be the same as that of Christ Jesus: Who, being in very nature God, did not consider equality with God something to be grasped, but made himself nothing, taking the very nature of a servant, being made in human likeness. And being found in appearance as a man, he humbled himself and became obedient to death—even death on a cross!"

Philippians 2:5-11 (NIV)

Jesus Christ is the ultimate servant of all time. In order to develop a servant's heart, we must first look deeply into the mind, heart and life of Jesus. Have you ever wondered why Jesus did it? Why did He make such an astounding choice to be a servant?

If you were given alternative options of money, fame and power at the start of your life, would you ultimately and actively choose to be a servant above all else? Few, if any of us would. But Jesus did. God in the flesh with free will and the ability to be whomever He desired chose to be a servant. Why?

One reason is that servant-hood is a characteristic of God. Colossians 2:9 (NIV) says, "For in Christ all the fullness of the Deity lives in bodily form." So when we look at Jesus, we see a mirror image of God. Person-ally, I find it hard to imagine God serving in any capacity. He alone is worthy to *receive* all service and give back nothing. Yet because of what we see in Jesus, we must acknowl-edge that part of His character and nature is servant-hood.

"Jesus chose to serve because that is simply who He is."

Imagine being invited to meet the President of the United States. You walk into the Oval Office and are introduced to him. After dismissing all his assistants, the President spends the next half hour serving you. He allows you to choose the chair of your choice. He pours you a glass of iced tea and asks if you'd like sugar in it. He asks you what you'd like to talk about. He gives you a spe-cial gift. Just as you're leaving, without request, he gives you the phone number of his private line to use in time of need. Outside his office, his secretary casually inquires, "How did things go?" You respond in disbelief, "Why did the President spend his time serving me?" She smiles knowingly and responds, "Because that is simply who he is."

Jesus chose to serve because that is simply who He is.

Jesus also chose to be a servant because He knew our greatest need and that He was the only one qualified to meet it. An excellent servant foresees the need of another and without request, takes care of it. A serving spouse for example, may foresee a spouse's need to get up and going in the morning. Without request, the spouse rises early each morning and prepares a fresh pot of hot coffee.

Jesus foresaw our need of forgiveness for our sins. The only way to meet it was to have a sinless person bear punishment for all the sins, of all sinners, of all time. He was the only One who could do it. He would have to humble Himself, leave His glory and position in heaven and come to earth in human likeness. The only way to meet the need was to become a servant Himself.

Jesus chose to be a servant because it was the only way to bring us back to our heavenly Father.

In order to develop a servant's heart we must concentrate intently on Jesus—the ultimate servant. We take on the characteristics of the things or the persons we choose to concentrate on. Consider the following story.

Located in the White Mountains of New Hampshire is a famous pass known as Franconia Notch. For thousands of years, protruding from its rocky walls was a granite formation resembling the profile of an old man peering intently over the valley. It was called "The Old Man of the Moun-

WEEK TWO

tain." Nathaniel Hawthorne drew his inspiration for "The Legend of the Great Stone Face" from that unusual rock formation.

Perhaps you know the story. A boy named Ernest lives in the valley from which he views daily a face fashioned in the mountain. His mother tells him that someday a venerable man bearing that image will visit the valley. Years go by. Great people from all walks of life come, but no one has the resemblance. Ernest reaches old age disappointed that he's not seen his mother's prediction fulfilled.

Finally, a renowned poet visits the area and listens to Ernest deliver a speech to his neighbors. The poet notices in Ernest's face the visage of the great stone face on the mountain. Having gazed on that figure daily for many years, Ernest, now a venerable old man, has gradually come to bear its image.

What are you focusing on? Whatever it is that you choose to spend your time, energy and resources on, that's what shapes you. So choose wisely. Choose Jesus. Place your undivided focus on Jesus. The more you allow His heart, mind and life to shine on you, the more you'll transform into His likeness—the likeness of a servant.

POINT TO PONDER

We take on the characteristics of the things we choose to concentrate on.

VERSE TO REMEMBER

"Your attitude should be the same as that of Christ Jesus."

Philippians 2:5 (NIV)

QUESTIONS TO CONSIDER

When you examine your own life, what is it that you're truly and honestly concentrating on? Does it reflect what you strive to become?

NOTES

LORDING IT OVER

"Jesus called them together and said, "You know that the rulers of the Gentiles lord it over them, and their high officials exercise authority over them. Not so with you. Instead, whoever wants to become great among you must be your servant, and whoever wants to be first must be your slave—just as the Son of Man did not come to be served, but to serve, and to give his life as a ransom for many."

Matthew 20:25-28 (NIV)

WEEK TWO

We're all born with a desire for greatness. At the center of our hearts is a craving for power, authority, influence and position. Most parents want this for their children too. Jesus' disciples and their parents were no different. Just prior to the above verses Matthew tells us, "Then the mother of Zebedee's sons came to Jesus with her sons and, kneeling down, asked a favor of him. 'What is it you want?' he asked. She said, 'Grant that one of these two sons of mine may sit at your right and the other at your left in your kingdom'" (Matthew 20:20-21, NIV).

The disciples had been living with and learning from Jesus for about three years. This was the moment they had been waiting for. In their minds, it was finally time to confront the local authorities. Jesus had even said the confrontation could result in loss of life. After witnessing Jesus' supernatural power and realizing He was the Son of God, they assumed it was time for Jesus to seize His rightful place of authority and replace the corrupt and abusive leaders. Of course, it was only fitting to assume that as His chosen followers, they too would attain their rightful place of authority. Finally, they would leave their lowly, unpredictable, nomadic lifestyle and seize what they longed for: *greatness*.

They couldn't have been more wrong. The disciples' faulty assumptions were based on an earthly understanding of power and authority—on what they saw and experienced each day. But Jesus knew greatness to be much more. Yes, a conflict was about to happen. Jesus was about to give them some dramatic news.

Two significant types of authority were prevalent in Jesus' day: governmental authority and the religious authority of the Jewish leaders. During this time, the Romans practically ruled the entire civilized world.

While Jews were allowed to maintain their autonomy, Roman officials kept a close eye on the Jewish community. Roman soldiers and officials made their presence highly visible in Jerusalem and the surrounding Israeli territories. They had a hierarchical form of government with distinct levels of authority. The higher the level, the more authority and power one possessed. "Greatness" was based on one's position. In Jesus' time, Emperor Tiberius was the Roman ruler and thought to be the greatest of all mankind. To further secure his "greatness," the emperor had his name and face inscribed on all currency and statues. He even

"Jesus crushed the disciples' faulty understanding and redefined greatness for us all."

commanded that people acknowledge his greatness by hailing his name and bowing down to him.

Judaism was also based on hierarchy. Religious leaders such as the Pharisees and Sadducees used their position to exercise authority over people. They manipulated Old Testament laws and wrote new ones to control people. If a woman (not a man) was caught in adultery, she was stoned to death (executed by throwing rocks at her). Religious leaders even participated in the execution.

The disciples too had been victims of this abuse of authority. They knew Jesus had what it took to become a different type of religious leader—One who would actually help the people. As witnesses to Jesus' supernatural power, they expected Jesus to replace the emperor and

WEEK TWO

seize rulership. The disciples knew their opportunity to achieve greatness was at hand.

With the disciples poised for earthly greatness, it was time for Jesus to clarify His plan and revise their definition. In Matthew 20:25-28, Jesus crushed the disciples' faulty understanding and redefined greatness for us all with three truths:

1. In our society, we define greatness as someone with authority *over* others. This is contradictory to God's plan.

2. God's definition of greatness is when you willingly position your self *under* others. You achieve greatness by being a servant and serving every person in your life.

3. Ultimately, the credibility of this definition rests on Jesus' flawless modeling of it, both on earth and throughout eternity. The supreme example of servant-hood is Jesus willingly giving His own life as a ransom payment for all of us who are held captive to sin and sin's punishment.

Do you want to be great? God wants you to be great. The only path to true greatness is through daily surrendering our old hearts, throwing away society's definitions and examples, and taking on a new heart through the teachings and example of Jesus.

POINT TO PONDER

Jesus' teaching about greatness is contradictory to society's understanding of greatness.

VERSE TO REMEMBER

"Whoever wants to become great among you must be your servant."
Matthew 20:26 (NIV)

QUESTIONS TO CONSIDER

Why does servant-hood involve a choice? What hurdles do you need to
overcome to live as a servant? Who, in your life, can you serve today?

WEEK TWO

NOTES

TAKING CARE OF BUSINESS

We're God's caretakers. He gives us time, talents and treasures to manage on His behalf, for His glory and for His benefit. Psalm 24:1 (NIV) says, "The earth is the LORD's, and everything in it, the world, and all who live in it." He created everything we see, touch, hear, smell or taste. It's all His. We are to use it for His glory. He is the reason for everything.

> *"His master replied, 'Well done, good and faithful servant! You have been faithful with a few things; I will put you in charge of many things. Come and share your master's happiness!'"*
>
> Matthew 25:21 (NIV)

We came into this world with nothing and we'll leave this world with nothing. The way we manage the resources He gives us while we're here on earth is extremely important to God. It will ultimately determine our heavenly responsibilities.

In Matthew 25:14-30, Jesus tells the parable of the talents. In this story, a master entrusts three of his servants with a number of talents before going on a journey. (A talent is a measure of money worth about one thousand dollars today.) Each servant received a different amount according to his abilities. When the master returned he settled his accounts with each of them. The first servant, entrusted with five talents, gained five more. The second ser-

"He expects you to use, expand and multiply these gifts according to the unique abilities He's blessed you with."

vant, entrusted with two talents, gained two more. The master praised both, saying, "Well done, good and faithful servant! You have been faithful with a few things; I will put you in charge of many things. Come and share your master's happiness!"

The third servant, entrusted with one talent, returned it to his master. The master replied, "You wicked, lazy servant! So you knew that I harvest where I have not sown and gather where I have not scattered seed? Well then, you should have put my money on deposit with the bankers, so that when I returned I would have received it back with interest. Take the talent from him and give it to the one who has the ten talents. For

everyone who has, will be given more and he will have an abundance. Whoever does not have, even what he has will be taken from him. And throw that worthless servant outside, into the darkness, where there will be weeping and gnashing of teeth" (Matthew 25:26-30, NIV).

At first glance, it may seem that the master was overly harsh with the third servant. But God generously entrusts each of us with resources of time, talent and treasures. He doesn't intend for you to simply hold on to them. He expects you to use, expand and multiply these gifts according to the unique abilities He's blessed you with. He wants you to use them not only for your own benefit or pleasure but also for His benefit. In doing so He'll reward you by entrusting you with even more.

The parable doesn't stop with our responsibility to expand our resources for His kingdom. It goes a step further by saying that failure to do so results in negative consequences. The Bible says, "And if you are untrustworthy about worldly wealth, who will trust you with the true riches of heaven? And if you are not faithful with other people's money, why should you be trusted with money of your own?" (Luke 16:11-12, NLT).

While this parable refers to money, the way we use our time and spiritual gifts or talents is just as important as how we use our money for His glory. God frowns upon laziness and wants us to use our spiritual gifts. He doesn't want to see them lie dormant.

Consider what you are doing with the resources God has entrusted to you. Are you using your God-given time, talents and treasures to honor Him? Would we be honoring God if we gave of our time but didn't share our spiritual gifts? Would we be honoring God if we gave of our time and our spiritual gifts but didn't share our treasures? And finally,

WEEK TWO

would God be honored if we gave of our treasures, but didn't share our time and talents? God wants us to give all three; He wants us to give of our time, talents and treasures. Besides, whose are they anyway?

POINT TO PONDER

We're God's stewards, caring for what He has entrusted to us.

VERSE TO REMEMBER

"...Well done, good and faithful servant! You have been faithful with a few things; I will put you in charge of many things. Come and share your master's happiness!" Matthew 25:21b (NIV)

QUESTIONS TO CONSIDER

Do you believe that your time, talents and treasures belong to God and are to be used for His glory? Why or why not? What can you do today to use them for His glory?

NOTES

BLUE VEST SERVING

When you woke up this morning, did you ask yourself: "How can I serve today? In my workplace, my church, my family, my daily interactions, how can I serve someone else today?" These are the questions a true servant is always asking. It's an others-focused attitude that lies at the core of a servant's heart. As Paul says in Philippians 2:3-4 (NIV), "Do nothing out of selfish ambition or vain conceit, but in humility consider

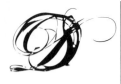

"Do nothing out of selfish ambition or vain conceit, but in humility consider others better than yourselves. Each of you should look not only to your own interests, but also to the interests of others."

Philippians 2:3-4 (NIV)

others better than yourselves. Each of you should look not only to your own interests, but also to the interests of others." Notice what Paul *isn't* saying. He's not saying, "Each of you should think less of yourselves." He's saying, "Think of yourself *less*. Don't be so focused on making sure all your needs, wants and desires are satisfied. Pay attention to the needs of others and go out of your way to serve them."

Self-less living is almost unthinkable in our world. We hear messages to the contrary like, "Look out for number one." "If you put others first you'll be left behind." "The only way to be happy is to have everything you want in life." And yet Paul is suggesting an entirely different way of living—a life modeled after the life of Jesus. As we've seen this past week, Jesus' life was marked by servant-hood in every encounter He experienced. He never passed up an opportunity to serve whether it was a person in need of healing or a child in need of loving attention. He seized those opportunities, even sought them out, and His servant lifestyle made an eternal difference in this world. As His followers, we're called to do the same.

Living the servant life can be difficult. It's radically different from the way most people approach their day. Instead of asking, "What can I *get* from life or others today?" we need to be asking, "What can I *give* to serve God and others?" This shift in attitude makes all the difference. It's using your life, gifts and resources to benefit others instead of using others to benefit you.

For many people, life is like a giant Wal-Mart. As the largest company in the world, Wal-Mart has mastered the art of meeting customers' needs. Each of their associates wear the trademark blue vest with the

WEEK TWO

words "How Can I Help You?" screen-printed across the back. Employees are trained to anticipate the needs of customers. The company is keenly aware that if they don't meet needs quickly and inexpensively, customers will take their business elsewhere.

This consumer attitude has become so much a part of our culture that people approach every dimension of life that way. They want to quickly and conveniently find what they want and get it at the lowest possible personal cost. Their lives are spent as consumers, focused on satisfying their own needs and often showing little concern for the needs of others. This attitude affects every facet of life. It can creep into relationships. People want fulfillment and companionship but are unwilling to make personal sacrifices to meet the needs of others. They're happy to be a friend or spouse on their own terms as long as it doesn't involve too much personal investment. The consumer attitude creeps into professional dealings as well. People exploit and manipulate for personal gain without any regard for the needs of others.

But of all places, this consumer attitude is most common and dangerous in church life. When people sense a spiritual need in their lives they come to the church expecting the community of Christians to meet their needs quickly and efficiently. Church staff and volunteers are treated as if wearing the familiar Wal-Mart vests; they're just there to help others find what they want and to do it with a smile. If their needs are met, the consumer attitude "customers" often return to normal life and ignore the church until they want help with some other need. When they feel their needs aren't being met, they simply choose to "take their business elsewhere" and bounce from church to church in search of a community that will cater completely to their needs and ask nothing in return. Since the "perfect" church doesn't exist, people with the consumer attitude often become disillusioned and withdraw from the community of believers.

This consumer mindset is opposite of the attitude Paul is talking about in Philippians 2. Followers of Jesus are to imitate Him, living their lives as servants. Instead of living life with a *consumer* mindset, Christ-followers learning to follow His example of servant-hood live their lives as *contributors*. Instead of expecting others to meet their needs, they set out to help meet the needs of others, contributing their gifts or resources in the process. Rather than

Instead of asking, "What I can I *get* from life or others today?" we need to be asking, "What can I *give* to serve God and others?"

approaching life like it's Wal-Mart, they put on the blue vest themselves and look for ways to serve.

Contributors don't wait to be asked. They spend the day looking for opportunities to serve others. It may be volunteering in a church ministry. It may mean taking an extra shift at work to give someone a chance to be with his or her family at a difficult time. It may mean helping out a single parent by offering to baby-sit or to meet a financial need. It may mean offering a pat on the back or encouragement to someone who needs it. These are simple acts of service, but each is an example of putting on the blue vest, asking yourself how you can serve today and living

WEEK TWO

life as a contributor rather than a consumer.

Being a contributor doesn't mean you never have times of need. Often the challenges of life are too great to handle alone and you'll need the help of others along the way. Learning to draw strength from those around you is key to living in our world. But constantly drawing from others without offering the same kind of help in kind is allowing the consumer mindset to guide your life. Instead, approach the day by slipping on the blue servant's vest and asking every moment, "How can I help?" Learning to be a servant in that way will begin to unlock the true fulfillment we're all looking for and help us as we learn to live like Jesus.

POINT TO PONDER

You have opportunities to be a servant every day.

VERSE TO REMEMBER

"Do nothing out of selfish ambition or vain conceit, but in humility consider others better than yourselves. Each of you should look not only to your own interests, but also to the interests of others."
Philippians 2:3-4 (NIV)

QUESTION TO CONSIDER

How different would your life and attitude be if you spent your day looking for opportunities to serve others?

NOTES

....

....

....

....

....

....

....

....

....

....

....

....

....

....

....

....

....

....

....

....

....

....

....

SECRET SERVICE

Pssst. Do you want to join the Secret Service? The Secret Service for God, that is. It'll cost you your time, your heart and sometimes your money, but the rewards are far greater than you could ever imagine. So great in fact, they extend beyond our earthly realm.

Jesus tells us in Matthew 6:1-4 to give to the needy and do acts of righteousness so that only God can see, not people. You see Jesus knows

"But when you give to the needy, do not let your left hand know what your right hand is doing, so that your giving may be in secret. Then your Father, who sees what is done in secret, will reward you."

Matthew 6:3-4 (NIV)

that when you purposely do something nice when no one's looking, you're not seeking recognition and so your heart is in the right place.

One of the most famous people who served the needy and poor was Mother Teresa. Although she won the Nobel Peace Prize in 1979 for her work, she remained truly humble her entire life. She offered her advice to us: "Speak tenderly to them. Let there be kindness in your face, in your eyes, in your smile, in the warmth of your greeting. Always have a cheerful smile. Don't only give your care, but give your heart as well."

Jesus isn't asking you to do something He didn't do. He gave His heart to the needy and poor all the time when He walked the earth. In Mark 1:40-45, Jesus is "filled with compassion" for a man with leprosy. Jesus healed the man and "sent him away with a strong warning: See that you don't tell this to anyone."

The more you serve in secret, the easier it becomes.

If you're like me, it's natural to want recognition or attention for doing something good for someone. I recently did a "good deed" for someone in secret. She called to tell me what happened, all the while speculating that it was someone from work who did it. In my excitement, it practically *killed* me not to exclaim, "It was me! I did it!"

Throughout the course of our conversation, I had to squelch that desire time and time again. But by keeping quiet, I learned something. The more you serve in secret, the easier it becomes. Practice makes perfect. And after you've perfected it and your heart truly becomes humble, you'll reap immeasurable rewards because God always keeps His promises.

WEEK TWO

DAY 12

It's normal for us to think about the rewards we may receive by doing good deeds. But earthly rewards such as success, money, material possessions or personal recognition are not as important to God. His rewards are given in other ways, both on this earth and in heaven.

Salvation is a free gift, and if you've truly accepted it, one day you'll be in heaven with our Lord. When we get there, 2 Corinthians 5:10 (NIV) states, "For we must all appear before the judgment seat of Christ, that each one may receive what is due him for the things done while in the body, whether good or bad." The motives of our works will be tested and God will know whether we did them for Him or for ourselves. Our lives in heaven will be determined by the sacrifices we make here on earth. And since we'll be in heaven for eternity, we'd be wise to make some sacrifices during our short time on earth.

If you still find it hard to serve secretly, get creative. If you put money in the offering so that your friends will see, start mailing in your check. Sneak away from your busy schedule one Saturday a month to volunteer with the homeless, but don't tell anyone. Leave some food by your neighbor's house, ring the doorbell and run! Have some fun with it! When you secretly serve for God, your heart will be filled with joy.

POINT TO PONDER

Serve in secret for God.

VERSE TO REMEMBER

"Then your Father, who sees what is done in secret, will reward you."

Matthew 6:4b (NIV)

QUESTIONS TO CONSIDER

How can you serve in God's "Secret Service" this week? Long term?

WEEK TWO

NOTES

FOR
HIRE

WANTED: Unsung hero for challenging position. Long hours, low pay, few promotions. Only people totally committed need apply.

Who wants a job like that? Most of us would skim right over that one and look for positions promising good money, frequent promotions, excellent benefits, paid sick leave, weeks of vacation time and great retirement plans.

"...I am among you as one who serves."

Luke 22:27b (NIV)

Despite your job or career, the Bible clearly states that as a Christ-follower you're called to serve. Saddleback Christian Church's Senior Pastor, Rick Warren, says, "If I have no love for others, no desire to serve

others, I should question whether Christ is really in my life." A non-serving Christian is a contradiction in terms. What you *are* is God's gift to you; what you *do* with yourself is your gift to God. Jesus modeled this perfectly in Luke 22:27b (NIV) by saying, "…I am among you as one who serves."

Jesus served unconditionally! Most of us wouldn't have a problem serving if we could choose whom and how we would serve. But Jesus demonstrated in John 13 that we're to serve unconditionally. That means even the difficult people in our lives. God's purpose for your life was not to have a selective heart for serving, but rather an unconditional heart to serve God's selective people. In other words, you were called by God to serve His people unconditionally! Put aside your shortcomings, personal opinions and selfish attitude. Put on the humility of Christ and commit to developing a servant's heart!

"A non-serving Christian is a contradiction in terms."

On day one of this devotional, we looked at Ephesians 2:10 (NIV) which says, "For we are God's workmanship, created in Christ Jesus to do good works, which God prepared in advance for us to do." Doing "good deeds" is your spiritual act of worship to God. Whenever you serve others with an unconditional heart, you're actually serving God and fulfilling His design and purpose for your life.

Jesus served faithfully! Jesus gathered His disciples together for one last time to celebrate the Passover Feast. He knew what the next 24 hours held in store for Him; a mock trial, sentencing and crucifixion. And yet, in the midst of it all, Jesus clothed Himself in the servant's towel, poured water into the washbasin and began to wash the disciples' feet. Jesus served faithfully, all the while knowing that before the night was over His closest and dearest friends and followers would scatter and disown Him. Peter would deny even knowing Him and Judas would betray Him with a kiss. But Jesus didn't change His mission even when His closest friends became cowards, traitors and difficult people. He continued to fulfill the purpose for which God had sent Him, not to be served, but to serve and give His life as a ransom.

Are you serving even God's difficult people faithfully like Jesus did? If you think this is a one-way street, consider this. Chances are you and I may be difficult people in other people's lives! Yet God uses imperfect people to do His perfect will. Take that first step toward serving like the "master servant" served: faithfully!

Jesus served equally! We all make lists to help us remember grocery items or tasks to complete. Unfortunately, some of us make mental lists about other people. We have lists of people we don't like, people who talk too much, selfish people, people who don't treat us the way we think we should be treated. All of these could be summarized into our "difficult people" list. All too often, we count these people off without giving it another thought. Negative lists prevent us from giving our best to God when it comes to serving His people. It's not our place to decide whom to serve based on how we feel about them. Galatians 6:3 (NLT) says, "If you think you are too important to help someone in need, you are only fool-

ing yourself. You are really a nobody." Read it again. That's convicting!

Jesus specialized in menial tasks that everyone else tried to avoid: washing feet, helping children, fixing breakfast and serving lepers. Nothing was beneath Him because He came to serve! He didn't see God's children as *difficult people*, but rather as *people with difficulties* who needed to be served. Only when we adopt the heart and attitude of Jesus can we begin to serve the way He did. Unconditionally! No strings attached! True servants don't make excuses. They enjoy helping people, meeting needs and doing ministry. They, "serve the Lord with gladness," despite the circumstances (Psalm 100:2a, KJV)! Remember, Jesus served unconditionally, faithfully and equally to everyone!

POINT TO PONDER

Jesus served unconditionally, faithfully and equally to everyone!

VERSE TO REMEMBER

"I am among you as one who serves." Luke 22:27b (NIV)

QUESTIONS TO CONSIDER

What are some of the obstacles or challenges preventing you from serving unconditionally, faithfully and equally? What tangible steps can you take to overcome them?

NOTES

BROKEN DREAMS

Gone were the dreams of love and acceptance as she tended to her three children. Moving through the motions just to get through the day, Tina paused for a second, glancing at the television. She'd seen the speaker often but never really listened to him. This time it was different. The words he spoke resonated in her mind like never before. It was time to move forward in life and make a change.

"My thoughts and my ways are higher than yours."
Isaiah 55:9 (CEV)

Months earlier there came a knock on the door. Uncharacteristically, she opened it and took time to listen to her visitor. She recognized the message he shared, for it was not new, but warm and familiar teachings

from her otherwise painful childhood. Tina knew there was a void in her life, her heart and her soul. But until that day, she had no idea how to fill the empty space. Listening to the words of a stranger, it suddenly all became clear.

Life-changing decisions may be made in a moment, but when the moment passes, you must take steps to move forward. She knew the only way to effect change was through Jesus, but getting started was difficult.

Tina had witnessed the power of God's love in her troubled past. She was born in Honduras and handed off to an aunt as her mother worked the streets. Abused at night by the family she once trusted, she was stripped of innocence and the joys of childhood. As the years passed, the abuse intensified, destroying any dreams of a normal and happy home life. Without her mother's love or a father to protect her, she found new hope at the church her neighbors introduced her to. There she discovered Christ's love and an escape from the increasingly ugly reality of life.

Tina's mother eventually came to her rescue. Now armed with a stable job, she built a new life for them. For the first time, Tina knew security. But with her external world stabilizing, Tina made new friends and soon drifted from God. Her constant search for love and acceptance only resulted in history repeating itself through a string of abusive boyfriends. Ultimately, Tina was kicked out of school and ostracized from friends. Then she discovered she was pregnant. Feeling rejected and alone, she wondered if this was all life had to offer. Suicide seemed a viable option. But her mother knew this was not the end for Tina. She sought to restart their lives in a new place: America.

A change in venue can do a lot of things but it can't erase what's

WEEK TWO

imprinted on your heart. Tina struggled to move forward but constantly wrestled with her past. She married and divorced within the year. She married again, had children and tried escaping her past through drugs and alcohol. She divorced again.

Then came that knock on the door. She found herself listening to long-forgotten teachings that had once brought her through the roughest times in her young life. Sensing a breakthrough, Tina again tried to break the strongholds of her heart and life. She married the man she was living with and began attending church. Still, her past clung to her like a homesick child. It wasn't about to let go. Failure and divorce ensued.

"Feeling rejected and alone, she wondered if this was all life had to offer. Suicide seemed a viable option."

But God wasn't giving up on Tina either. Again, He came knocking at her heart's door, this time through a powerful television ministry. She finally realized she couldn't do it on her own. Only through God could she truly bring change in her life.

Tina found a church where she and her family felt welcome and comfortable. She started reading the Bible and attending a small group, and was mentored and taught by godly women about being a good mother and wife. As she rediscovered God's love and acceptance, she once again found the hope she'd embraced as a child. As she grew to understand God had never forsaken her, she recalled the many times He

intervened throughout her painful struggles. She began to heal and her faith grew strong.

As Tina grew in her walk with God, she involved her children at church too. By doing so, she discovered her own place to help others. In Children's Ministries, she cared for little ones and comforted crying babies. No longer did she only care about herself and her family. She experienced joy and fulfillment like she'd never had. The more she gave of herself, the more joy she experienced in return.

The journey from brokenness to fulfillment took nine years of growth and change. Today, Tina is using her experiences to make a difference in the lives of hurting people. As a volunteer, she meets with bruised and broken people who are looking for food and financial assistance. Tina offers hope far beyond the physical sustenance they are seeking. Like the people who led by example in her own life by helping her move forward with Christ, she now leads a small group and helps others find healthy relationships in spite of their past.

Do you ever think that only a person raised in the church who has always walked with God can lead a small group or be a mentor? Like Tina, your past experiences might be the breakthrough that can help someone else navigate through similar struggles, temptations or failures. Yes, God does incredible things through brokenness. Will you let Him use yours?

WEEK TWO

POINTS TO PONDER

1. There is hope when you're looking for love and acceptance.

2. Share with others the hope you've discovered in your walk with God.

3. When you stop focusing on yourself, God will take you to a whole new level.

VERSE TO REMEMBER

"My thoughts and my ways are higher than yours." Isaiah 55:9 (CEV)

QUESTIONS TO CONSIDER

Are you focusing more on God or yourself? What tangible steps can you take to find the level of fulfillment that God intends for you?

NOTES

....

....

....

....

....

....

....

....

....

....

....

....

....

....

....

....

....

....

....

....

....

WEEK TWO

DISCOVERING YOUR GIFTS

"Each one should use whatever gift he has received to serve others, faithfully administering God's grace in its various forms."

1 Peter 4:10 (NIV)

DAY 15

ICONS, GIANTS AND YOU

Have you ever watched someone so good at what he or she does, it just looks easy and natural? You think, "This is that person's purpose. This is what he or she was born to do." Think about Tiger Woods hitting a golf ball, Mozart composing, Michelangelo painting or sculpting, Hitchcock directing or Mother Teresa helping people in need. The list is

"Before I made you in your mother's womb, I chose you. Before you were born, I set you apart for a special work."
Jeremiah 1:5 (NCV)

endless. Some people are so skilled and talented, so natural and gifted, they've become icons. Their names are synonymous with what they do. You can't imagine them doing anything else.

WEEK THREE

The Bible is full of examples as well, like Abraham as the father of faith, Moses as Israel's first leader and 'friend of God', David as a king 'after God's own heart', Esther as the queen who saves her people, Stephen as the first martyr, Barnabas as the great encourager, Peter as the rock the Church was built on, Paul as the missionary to the Gentiles, and of course, Jesus, crucified and risen to forgive our sins. Every one of these spiritual giants lived to fulfill God's purpose for their lives. They did what they were born to do.

You can probably think of people in your own life who were naturally gifted in a way that impacted you. Maybe you had a teacher who inspired you, a boss or co-worker who lived a life of integrity or a parent who never gave up on you. Some people serve so beautifully and effortlessly, you just know that whatever they're doing is their purpose in life. It's what they were born to do. Spiritually speaking, this is absolutely true. As a Christ-follower, it's true for you too.

In 2 Timothy 1:9 (LB), Paul tells us, "It is he who saved us and chose us for his holy work." Peter expands on this thought saying, "God has given gifts to each of you from his great variety of spiritual gifts. Manage them well so that God's generosity can flow through you." 1 Peter 4:10 (NLT) When we were saved, we were spiritually born-again. When we serve God and others, we're doing what we were *born-again* to do.

In Jeremiah, God declares, "Before I made you in your mother's womb, I chose you. Before you were born, I set you apart for a special work" (Jeremiah 1:5, NCV). He later says, "I know the plans I have for you . . ." (Jeremiah 29:11, NIV). In Psalm 139, King David wrote, "My frame was not hidden from you when I was made in the secret place. .

. All the days ordained for me were written in your book before one of them came to be."

As we discussed last week, God has a plan for you. He didn't create you and then turn His back on you. He is actively and intimately involved in your life. He gives your life purpose. And He's given you gifts to fulfill that purpose. God's plan for you is simple; serve Him by serving others. Colossians 3:23 (NIV) says, "Whatever you do, work at it with all your heart, as working for the Lord . . ." God wants you to discover and use the spiritual gifts He's given you in order to serve Him and others. In his book, *The Purpose Driven Life*, Rick Warren defines spiritual gifts as "special God-empowered abilities for serving (God and others) that are given only to believers." In 1 Corinthians 12:7, Paul informs us that spiritual gifts are "given to each of us as a means to helping the entire church."

> "God's plan for you is simple; serve Him by serving others."

You may not think you could ever do anything as well as Tiger Woods hitting a golf ball or Mozart composing an opera. You may not think of yourself as a Moses or a David when it comes to serving God. But the awesome truth is, God created you, chose you and gifted you for the purpose of serving Him and others. So where do your gifts and abilities lie? Remember those people who impacted your life in a positive way? Whose life can you impact today? How can you make a difference in someone's life tomorrow, by what you do today?

WEEK THREE

POINT TO PONDER

Using your spiritual gifts is what you were *born-again* to do.

VERSE TO REMEMBER

"God has given gifts to each of you from his great variety of spiritual gifts. Manage them well so that God's generosity can flow through you." 1 Peter 4:10 (NLT)

QUESTIONS TO CONSIDER

What talents and abilities do you have? How can you use them to serve others and fulfill God's purpose for your life?

NOTES

WE ARE FAMILY

Have you ever heard someone say, "I believe in Jesus, but I'm not sure I believe in organized church." Maybe you've even said it yourself. Comments like this are usually rooted in past experiences. If someone feels disappointed, let down or even betrayed by a pastor, a priest or a church member, they often distrust and ultimately disconnect from

> *"Now you are the body of Christ and each one of you is a part of it."*
> 1 Corinthians 12:27

church. Sadly, too many people turn their back on the church or "organized religion" after a negative or hurtful experience. They opt instead for a "private relationship" with Jesus.

This may sound harsh, but a private relationship with Jesus apart from other believers is completely false and contradictory to the Bible. Now don't get me wrong. It's essential for all believers to have a private and personal side to their relationship with Jesus. But the personal side is deeply rooted in the context of community with other believers.

The New Testament describes believers as being part of a family or a body. You don't have a choice in the matter. When you became connected to Christ you automatically became connected to His family or His body. A "private" or "lone ranger" follower of Christ is completely unheard of in the New Testament. Certainly, the family you've joined in Christ has its odd quirks and negative qualities. Relationships in this family can be messy. The lingering effects of sin in the lives of Christ-followers can be expressed in hurtful ways. But God loves this family. Jesus died for this family. And God desires to use this family to show His love to the world.

In 1 Corinthians 12:12-26, Paul describes the family of God as a body. He says, "The body is a unit, though it is made up of many parts; and though its parts are many, they form *one body*." And, "For we were all baptized by *one Spirit* into *one body* — whether Jews or Greeks, slave or free — and we were all given the *one Spirit* to drink" (1 Corinthians 12:12-13, NIV). His message is clear. We're all linked together as one unit or body in Christ. <u>The Message</u> version puts it this way:

You can easily enough see how this kind of thing works by looking no further than your own body. Your body has many parts — limbs, organs, and cells — but no matter how many parts you can name, you're still one body. It's exactly the same with Christ. By

WEEK THREE

means of his one spirit, we all said goodbye to our partial and piecemeal lives. We used to independently call our own shots, but then we entered into a large and integrated life in which *he* has the final say in everything. (This is what we proclaimed in word and action when we were baptized.) Each of us is now a part of his resurrected body, refreshed and sustained at one fountain—his Spirit—where we all come to drink. The old labels we once used to identify ourselves, labels like Jew or Greek, slave or free—are no longer useful. We need something larger, more comprehensive. (1 Corinthians 12:12-13, MSG)

All of us who follow Jesus are now a part of a body or family that is larger and more comprehensive than our individual lives. Like it or not, we're connected to each other. We're not out on our own calling the shots, but rather part of a larger community following the direction of our leader, Jesus. A couple of truths emerge from this connection.

"A private relationship with Jesus apart from other believers is completely false and contradictory to the Bible."

1. **You need the body.** Because God created you to be a part of this body, you need all the different parts. Consider your own body. You need your eyes, ears, feet, hands, everything! Ask any disabled person. They miss using the body part they lost. The

spiritual correlation is just as strong. You need all the parts to operate at your optimal level.

2. **The body needs you.** The body of Christ is out of balance if you're not doing your part. Paul continues in 1 Corinthians 12 saying, "If the foot should say, 'Because I am not a hand, I do not belong to the body,' it would not for that reason cease to be a part of the body. And if the ear should say, 'Because I am not an eye, I do not belong to the body,' it would not for that reason cease to be part of the body. If the whole body were an eye, where would the sense of hearing be? If the whole body were an ear, where would the sense of smell be?" (1 Corinthians 12:15-17, NIV). Paul is saying that each of us has an important part to play in the body of Christ. If we fail to do our part, the body of Christ suffers. We are sorely missed.

Paul concludes his thoughts by saying, "You are Christ's body that's who you are! You must never forget this. Only as you accept your part of that body does your 'part' mean anything" (1 Corinthians 12:27, MSG).

WEEK THREE

POINT TO PONDER

When you became a Christian, you became a member of God's family and a vital part of the body of Christ.

VERSE TO REMEMBER

"Now you are the body of Christ and each one of you is a part of it." 1 Corinthians 12:27 (NIV)

QUESTIONS TO CONSIDER

What specifically are you doing to contribute to the overall health and well being of the body of Christ? What do you need to change to help the body function better?

NOTES

IGNORANCE IS BLISS

I love my mom. She's bright, articulate, accomplished and respected among her peers. She's reached the highest levels of responsibility and influence in her chosen field of politics. But when it comes to figuring out her VCR or computer, she's completely ignorant. In this area of life, *ignorance is bliss*. It's easier to call her son than figure it out herself.

"A spiritual gift is given to each of us as a means of helping the entire church."

Ephesians 2:10 NIV

When it comes to serving God, many of us enjoy the *ignorance is bliss* excuse too. Because we don't know what the different spiritual gifts are, it's easier to let someone else figure out how to serve God. But if you're committed to being a devoted Christ-follower, you can't claim ignorance. The Bible says, "Now about spiritual gifts, brothers, I do not want you to be ignorant." 1 Corinthians 12:1 (NIV)

Before reading further, be warned! Below is a description of many of the spiritual gifts listed in the Bible. Once you know them, you're responsible for what you know! You'll no longer be able to claim ignorance.

Congratulations! By reading on you're accepting the challenge to learn about spiritual gifts. First, a spiritual gift is the *special ability, given by the Holy Spirit, to accomplish the service God has called you to*. Four major biblical passages, Romans 12, 1 Corinthians 12, Ephesians 4 and 1 Peter 4, list at least 19 different spiritual gifts, but they're not meant to be exhaustive lists. Other spiritual gifts are mentioned in the Bible but these fit in the context of serving God and serving others:

Administration: The divine ability to understand what makes an organization or group function and the God given ability to develop and implement structures and processes, which make the organization more efficient and effective.

Discernment: The spiritual ability to distinguish between good and evil, right and wrong.

Encouragement: The divine ability to use God's truth to bring courage to those who are physically, spiritually or emotionally struggling.

Evangelism: The God given ability to engage nonbelievers with the truth of the gospel in a way that often moves them along in their spiritual journey.

Faith: The spiritual ability to trust in God's promises and direction with great steadfastness and confidence.

WEEK THREE

Giving: The God given ability to give away your time, talent and treasure in order to help others and to further the work of the kingdom of God.

Helps: The God given ability to see needs and the spiritual inclination to meet those needs in a way that serves others and furthers the work of the ministry.

Hospitality: The spiritual ability to care for others by offering personal and physical resources such as your home, food, personal presence, etc.

Intercession: The divine ability to pray specifically, consistently and powerfully for the needs of others.

Knowledge: The God given ability to bring the truth of God's word to the forefront of the life of an individual, group or church.

Leadership: The divine ability to see the big picture, communicate vision and to inspire and lead people to accomplish a goal or purpose for the kingdom of God.

Mercy: The spiritual ability to offer compassion, empathy and care to those who are suffering or are in need.

Prophecy: The God given ability to proclaim truth, confront falsehood and exhort others to live their lives in accordance with God's word.

Pastoring: The divine ability to give care, nurturing, direction and instruction to help a group of people grow in their walk with Christ.

Serving: The God given desire to meet practical needs as they arise. People with the gift of serving have a strong passion to be helpful in meeting specific needs in the lives of individuals or in the overall ministry of the church.

Teaching: The spiritual ability to accurately understand and communicate the truth of God's word to others in a way that motivates and challenges them to learn and grow.

Wisdom: The God given ability to apply the truth of God's word in a way that sheds light on specific circumstances and events in their own life and in the lives of others.

There's a key to using spiritual gifts correctly. First, Paul tells us not to plead ignorance when it comes to

> "If you're committed to being a devoted Christ-follower, you can't claim ignorance."

spiritual gifts. Then, in 1 Corinthians chapters 12 and 13, he continues by giving us a list of such gifts and saying:

> And now I will show you the most excellent way. If I speak in the tongues of men and of angels, but have not love, I am only a resounding gong or a clanging cymbal. If I have the gift of prophesy and can fathom all mysteries and all knowledge, and if I have a faith that can move mountains, but have not love, I am nothing. If I give all I possess to the poor and surrender my body to the flames, but have not love, I gain nothing.
> (1 Corinthians 12:31b -13:1-4, NIV)

Did you get it? Love is the key. Paul continues to write about using spiritual gifts in the most famous biblical chapter about love—the one you so often hear at weddings: "Love is patient, love is kind," etc. Isn't

it interesting? This chapter about how love expresses itself is all in the context of spiritual gifts and serving! God gives us gifts. He expects us to use them with an attitude of love.

So now you know. You can no longer claim ignorance. As a believer in Christ you have at least one, maybe more, of these gifts. God wants you to use them.

POINT TO PONDER

Ignorance is never an excuse for not developing your spiritual gifts.

VERSE TO REMEMBER

"A spiritual gift is given to each of us as a means of helping the entire church." 1 Corinthians 12:7 (NLT)

QUESTIONS TO CONSIDER

What steps have you taken to discover your spiritual gifts? What's keeping you from using them?

NOTES

BUT WAIT, THERE'S MORE!

Once you accept the gift of Jesus, you get salvation and so much more! God throws in the promise of eternal life in heaven, the grace to forgive your sins, and as if that weren't enough, a spiritual gift to boot. That's right, every Christian receives at least one gift. It's an amazing offer! Who could refuse?

"There are different kinds of gifts, but the same Spirit. There are different kinds of service but the same Lord. There are different kinds of working, but the same God works all of them in all men."

1 Corinthians 12:4-6 (NIV)

In 1 Corinthians 12:1 Paul says, "Now about spiritual gifts, brothers, I do not want you to be ignorant." He later continues with, "There are different kinds of gifts, but the same Spirit. There are different kinds of service but the same Lord. There are different kinds of working, but the same God works all of them in all men" (1 Corinthians 12:4-6, NIV). Paul emphasizes the unique diversity of our gifts, the importance of our giftedness and the unity of serving God through our gifts. God designed us to work together building the kingdom, to serve in our church and community and to learn to be more like Him.

So what are these gifts? A spiritual gift is a special ability the Holy Spirit gives to each believer upon accepting Christ. Your gift enables you to minister to others and build up the body of Christ. Gifts are a precious expression of God's love. Your spiritual gift or gifts represent God's purpose for you. God chose your gift(s). It's exactly what He wanted you to have. "But each man has his own gift from God; one has this gift, another has that" (1 Corinthians 7:7, NIV). God divinely provides diversity and interdependence on each other. Working together and using our gifts provides unity. It puts many gifts into action for Him.

So how can you discover your spiritual gifts?

1. Pray. Ask God to guide you in finding the best way for you. Ask Him to help you discover and use the unique gifts He's given you. Read the books of Ephesians and Corinthians, where spiritual gifts are referenced many times. Review yesterday's devotional and read the lists of gifts found in 1 Corinthians 12:1-11 and 27-31, Ephesians 4:11-12, Romans 12:3-8 and 1 Peter 4:9-11.

WEEK THREE

2. Ask a trusted Christian friend, a family member or a pastor what spiritual gifts he or she sees in you. Sometimes it's difficult to see your own gifts but it may be obvious to those around you. They can pray with you and reflect on how they've seen Christ working through you and where you seem most fulfilled. Your life experiences and spiritual background, combined with work and educational history, create your unique shape and design. But, spiritual gifts are much more than that; they give you a purpose and shape your ministry so you then have the privilege of serving and giving back to God what He's given you.

"Gifts are a precious expression of God's love."

3. Take a Spiritual Gifts assessment. Ask a pastor for a reliable gift assessment to help you discover your spiritual gift(s). Watch your church bulletin for a spiritual gifts seminar or class to help guide you in this journey. It'll help you explore your gifts, time, talent and treasures from God along with your personality and passions to help you discover where He gifted you to serve Him.

4. Visit a Christian bookstore or explore the Internet for Christian books or websites on discovering your spiritual gifts. Some Christian websites even offer an online spiritual gift assessment. They

typically provide an assessment tool, a subsequent analysis and an explanation of your gifts.

5. Consider how you're wired. What do you love to do? Are you an extrovert or introvert? Do you like working with people, accomplishing tasks or both? If you're task-oriented, consider behind-the-scenes involvement. If you prefer organizational or leadership roles, look for the up-front serving opportunities. Try serving in different areas and see what brings you joy and fulfillment. It's a discovery process; try it on and find your fit. You'll know the right one; it's the place you feel energized and are excited at the prospect of going back again.

6. Get started! Just by getting involved you may discover an aspect of ministry you really love or a way to serve you never considered. What are you passionate about? What do you have the heart to do for Christ? Pray about the groups or types of people you care about or have concerns for: teenagers, young children, homeless people or others. Our gifts so often line up with our passions. Check into community outreach that fits your passions. Seek serving opportunities that fit your passions, preferences and interests. Your gifts will shine through when you're serving where your passions lie.

You're here for a reason. There's a purpose for your life and God gifted you to accomplish that purpose. Discovering and using your gifts

will bring you incredible joy, fulfillment and satisfaction as you faithfully serve Him.

POINT TO PONDER

There's a purpose for your life and God gifted you to accomplish that purpose.

VERSE TO REMEMBER

"There are different kinds of gifts, but the same Spirit. There are different kinds of service, but the same Lord. There are different kinds of working, but the same God works all of them in all men."
1 Corinthians 12:4-6 (NIV)

QUESTIONS TO CONSIDER

Which of the above six steps have you taken to discover and use your spiritual gifts? What's the next step for you?

NOTES

MONKEY WITH A RED SHOE

My grandson and I love to play "I Spy." When we're sitting in a restaurant waiting for dinner or walking through a department store we immediately begin searching for unique or odd items we can use to start the game. He usually begins with something like, "I spy a monkey with a red shoe..." and the game is on. We can spend an entire dinner at

"And whatever you do, whether in word or deed, do it all in the name of the Lord Jesus, giving thanks to God the Father through him."

Colossians 3:17 (NIV)

a restaurant playing the game, which doesn't make us very good dinner companions, but we have great fun. Let me give you a little advice about playing "I Spy." The best items to use are those small, almost insignificant things in plain view. When the monkey with the red shoe is a little picture on the dinner menu, then you're playing the game the way it should be played.

The "I Spy" game has a lot in common with serving God. Our lives are filled with opportunities to serve God. It's our job to spy them out. Some serving opportunities are obvious. When we read the church bulletin and see that people are needed in traffic ministry or that the Women's Ministry needs people to help make phone calls, those are obvious needs. But other serving opportunities are more inconspicuous and subtle. Much like in "I Spy," serving God can be the most fun when it's something so small and insignificant you barely notice it as you walk about in your everyday life.

This is a game you can play with God, anywhere you are, no matter what you're doing. Colossians 3:17 (NIV) teaches us, "...whatever you do, whether in word or deed, do it all in the name of the Lord Jesus, giving thanks to God the Father through him." God calls us to serve Him through our words and deeds wherever we are or whatever we're doing. So as you move through your day, begin a little game of "I Spy" with God. Instead of a monkey with a red shoe, look for little opportunities to serve God in everyday life. God has some small, seemingly insignificant places for us to serve Him. Our part of the game is to find them. This isn't the kind of serving that requires a special spiritual gift. These are simple opportunities requiring little more than discernment to see the need, a dose of humility and the willingness to serve God. When you're putting gas in the car or shopping in the grocery store, start the game.

WEEK THREE

When you're taking the kids to school or having lunch with co-workers, start the game.

Now before you start thinking this is a child's game, let's review the rules: "Whatever you do, whether in word or deed, do it all in the name of the Lord Jesus, giving thanks." Those are some heavy rules to follow. It means when you're disciplining your child, you should play the game. "I spy an opportunity to serve You when I discipline my child with my words and deeds and give thanks to Jesus also." It means when your annoying brother-in-law is coming over to dinner, you should play the game. "I spy an opportunity to serve You in how I think, speak and act toward my annoying brother-in-law. And, oh yes, give thanks too."

"Our lives are filled with opportunities to serve God. It's our job to spy them out."

I told you it isn't always easy. You have a multitude of opportunities to serve God every day in the routine of life. So if you're ready to take the challenge, consider some of the ways you can play "I Spy" with God today.

POINT TO PONDER

God doesn't love you more when you serve Him, nor will His love diminish when you miss an opportunity to serve. This is a simple game of "I Spy" with your Daddy in Heaven.

VERSE TO REMEMBER

"And whatever you do, whether in word or deed, do it all in the name of the Lord Jesus, giving thanks to God the Father through him."
Colossians 3:17 (NIV)

QUESTIONS TO CONSIDER

How can you serve God in small ways during the course of your daily routine? How do you serve God already in little ways by the way you think, speak and act? How many ways are you missing? What's stopping you from serving God in the little ways?

WEEK THREE

NOTES

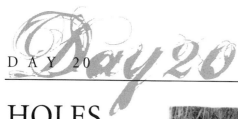

HOLES

Unfulfilled needs. Overworked and burnt-out volunteers. Too few people trying to meet the needs of many. Holes. This is a common condition of our world, our communities and our churches, but it needn't be. Holes shouldn't exist, not just for an ideal world, but in God's eyes as

> *"...choose seven men from among you who are known to be full of the Spirit and wisdom. We will turn this responsibility over to them..."*
>
> Acts 6:3 (NIV)

well. There are so many Christians to fill these needs, so many places to put a servant's heart to use.

Like the church, all communities can be viewed as a body with parts

WEEK THREE

that work together to function best. God would love for each community to be complete—no holes, no malfunctions and no needs unmet. Too often there's something inside us preventing this ideal. It may be a case of extreme pride. We think we're too good to help in areas needed. Maybe we have too many things on our plate to take the time to help out. Maybe we believe it's our government or community's job to ensure these things get done. In reality, it's your job and mine. Each of us, as citizens of heaven and earth, must unite as one and meet the needs of those less fortunate. In Matthew 14:13-21, Jesus spends the day teaching a crowd of people. Realizing it's dinnertime, He feeds the crowd with five loaves of bread and two fish. It's worth a quick read through to refresh your memory. Do you know what's interesting to me about this story? Christ enlightens His devoted (yet slightly dense) disciples on one of the not-so-mysterious mysteries of how the church and Christianity function.

Picture Jesus' emotional state. He's just finished an intense prayer time with the Father. He's still grieving the brutal execution of His beloved cousin. Just when the Father fills His soul, here come the droves of people that show up wherever He goes. As usual, they don't just come to say, "Hi, Jesus. How are you doing?" No, they have needs and concerns to tend to. The impromptu service lasts into the evening with the disciples finally suggesting He send these people home for dinner. But Jesus, in His supreme wisdom, says, "Forget that. These people are part of the church. You guys feed them."

At this point the disciples are thinking just about everything under the sun *except* how to feed these people. They likely thought, "Hey, we've been helping these people all day. Why can't someone else do it? We've got other things to do." Nevertheless, Jesus looked to them as if to say, "These people are your people; care for your sheep." The disciples found some food, gave it to Jesus and the rest is history.

The question is, after Jesus left them, could the disciples continue this feat, to lead a world and meet its needs? The answer is in Acts 4:32-35. The church becomes the nucleus of the community by sharing all they had with others. Why? They decided to focus completely on God and realized it's everyone's job to see that needs are met.

Now, flash-forward to Acts 6:1-7. Some of the widows in the church community are overlooked in the distribution of food. With a history of taking responsibility for the condition of the church, the apostles now take ownership of the problem. They appoint seven church members to ensure the widows' needs are met daily. Now pause to consider before you just skip over that. The implications are huge! No longer do people have to walk through life alone and feel left out. Your spiritual walk is not meant to be a solo journey but a group expedition. This is not only a great reason to join a small group; it's a great reason to serve! How many times have you thought something was wrong with the world? How often are you more likely to criticize than lend a helping hand? It's your world, your community, your church and your brothers and sisters in need. It's time to fill the holes, wherever they may be.

"God would love for each community to be complete, no holes, no malfunctions and no needs unmet."

WEEK THREE

POINT TO PONDER

It's your duty and mine to serve others so no one is in need.

VERSE TO REMEMBER

"Choose seven men from among you who are known to be full of the Spirit and wisdom. We will turn this responsibility over to them..."
Acts 6:3 (NIV)

QUESTIONS TO CONSIDER

What needs have you seen around you? What part can you play to help fill them?

NOTES

THAT'S JUST HOW GOD MADE ME

The first time I met Mark, I knew he was unlike anyone I'd ever met. I've never known such a hyperactive twenty-something-year-old. He can't pay attention for more than five seconds. Still, we hit it off right away. Mark is easy to talk to and open about things. He loves to laugh

> *"For you created my inmost being; you knit me together in my mother's womb."*
>
> Psalm 139:13 (NIV)

and can be pretty loud. So when I learned he enjoys volunteering in Junior High Ministry, it didn't surprise me. I could see him relating well with junior high students. He probably has a lot in common with them.

Over time, I've gotten to know Mark pretty well. We've talked about his ministry with Junior High. For me, working with these students is sheer insanity. It's just not my thing. But when I asked Mark about it, he said, "I'm a guy in my twenties with a twelve-year-old personality. That's just how God made me. Working with junior high students comes naturally to me. I've tried serving in other areas but this fits me perfectly."

My friendship with Mark reminds me that God created us all in a unique way. Of course, that's obvious in looking at our external or physical attributes. But we're also unique on the inside. Psalm 139:13 (NIV) says, "For you created my inmost being; you knit me together in my mother's womb." Our Creator determined each individual personality, or "inner wiring" as some would say, before we were even born. Our uniqueness developed inside our mother's womb.

One reason God made us unique is because He's unique Himself. God is unlike anyone or anything you've ever seen. In Exodus 3, God comes to Moses in a burning bush. Have you ever seen a bush that's on fire, but not really burning? Ever had a conversation with one? How's that for unique? God used Moses to lead His people out of slavery. Moses didn't have a gift for public speaking. He lacked confidence. But Moses allowed God to use him in a powerful way. God gave him a partner, Moses' brother Aaron, to do the public speaking. Together Moses and Aaron, each with his own unique gifts and talents, allowed God to use them to free His people.

God continues to reveal His unique personality and way of doing things throughout the Bible. In Joshua 6:3-5, God tells Joshua to march around the walls of Jericho blowing trumpets for six days. That's an

WEEK THREE

interesting strategy for defeating your enemy! In John 13:1-17, Jesus takes on the role of servant by washing His disciples' feet. The Son of God and Lord of All, washing twelve pairs of gritty, dirty, calloused feet? Can you think of any esteemed leader who would willingly take on that role today? Yes, God is truly unique and created each of us in a unique way too.

How has God made you? Are you organized or haphazard? Are you intentional or spontaneous? Are you laid back or energetic? So how will you allow God to use you? We're all wired differently. Some, like my friend Mark, have a personality perfect for working with junior high students. Others have gifts of organizing, teaching, planning, public speaking or any number of things. All of us are different in *how* we were made, yet are the same in *why* we were made.

"That's just how God made me. I've tried serving in other areas but this fits me perfectly."

Matthew 28:18-20 (NIV) says, "Then Jesus came to them and said, "All authority in heaven and on earth has been given to me. Therefore go and make disciples of all nations, baptizing them in the name of the Father and of the Son and of the Holy Spirit, and teaching them to obey everything I have commanded you. And surely I am with you always, to the very end of the age." No matter what our personality or uniqueness, we're all called to do one thing: make disciples. How are you using your uniqueness? Are you making disciples? Use your unique, one-of-a-kind personality to serve God. Take what God gave you and use it for Him. Be like my friend Mark and take advantage of your uniqueness!

POINT TO PONDER

All of us are different in how we were made yet are the same in why we were made.

Verse to Remember

"For you created my inmost being; you knit me together in my mother's womb." Psalm 139:13 (NIV)

QUESTIONS TO CONSIDER

In what ways has God made you unique? How are you using your God-given uniqueness to serve Him?

WEEK THREE

NOTES

WEEK 4

LOOKING IN THE MIRROR

"But in fact God has arranged the parts in the body, every one of them, just as he wanted them to be."

1 Corinthians 12:18 (NIV)

YOU'VE GOT PERSONALITY!

If you're ever feeling down or need a reminder of God's love for you, read Psalm 139. It says God knows you intimately. He's familiar with all your ways. He's with you in your highest of highs and your lowest of lows. He knit you together before you were even part of your mother's

> *"I will praise You, for I am fearfully*
> *and wonderfully made; Marvelous are*
> *Your works, And that my soul knows*
> *very well."*
>
> Psalm 139:14 (NKJV)

thoughts. You are fearfully and wonderfully made. Your days are ordained. You were created for purpose.

When I ponder Psalm 139 it overwhelms me, relieves me, excites me

WEEK FOUR

and as the Nicole Nordeman song, <u>Tremble</u>,* reminds, it causes me to tremble. Just let it sink in. God made you an original. There's no one else like you in the world. There never has been and never will be.

Recently, there's been a baby boom of boys among my friends and colleagues. Each new baby brought out a natural tendency in me to compare and look for resemblances in his parents and siblings. Of course there were similarities but quite simply and refreshingly, the baby looked purely like himself. Each child is a never-to-be-repeated combination of traits, absolutely unique and a miraculous marvel of God's designer genes. Each is his own person with his own personality, complete with likes and dislikes, sense of humor and sensitivities. Everything from what makes him tick, to what makes him sick. In time we'll glimpse from the outside what is already designed on the inside. We'll associate some of his preferences and behaviors to his environment, but he is simply re-fining how God has already wired him. He's developing his personality.

For the next few days we'll look at different personalities and how yours plays a critical role in how you can be used by and for God. We'll examine how your personality helps you choose where and how you serve and the kind of influence you can have.

Each personality consists of deep and unique mental preferences and habits. What you observe in behavior is the outward expression of those mental aerobics. Want a fun study in behavior? Pay attention at the airport the next time you travel; watch the checkout line at the grocery store; observe the urgent care waiting room or your child's classroom. A smaller group such as you and your spouse, you and your children or you and your coworkers might even be more interesting. Some people

behave similarly to you, some are totally opposite, and some are just plain weird. Learning to understand how we're wired from the inside helps us to better understand our own personalities. In doing so, we also gain insight into the personalities of those around us. This can be one of the most challenging, rewarding and ultimately God-honoring things you can do.

Have you ever tried jump-starting a car battery and mistakenly put the positive cable on the negative charge? It's not pretty. The same thing happens with personalities; some combinations just plain blow up. Why? Is one person wrong? Not necessarily. Each person thinks and behaves differently. Neither is wrong, but neither understands the other. When you seek to understand why people consistently and predictably behave the way they do, you can form a relationship that has charge but isn't going to blow up.

"When you seek to understand why people consistently and predictably behave the way they do, you can form a relationship that has charge but isn't going to blow up."

When you flip a light switch, you expect it to work. You don't think about the electrical system, the breaker box, the electric company (except when you pay the bill) or the power plant. Your house is simply wired so when you flip a switch, your expectations are met. People are like that. God designed your wiring a certain way. You have buttons and

WEEK FOUR

switches that generate normal and predictable responses. When other people say they "know you" or "understand you" they've pressed the buttons enough to learn your patterns of behavior. Some people are easier to read than others. Until you really know or understand someone, certain behaviors can frustrate, infuriate and drive you crazy. But since our entire lives are based on relationships with each other, it's to our advantage to minimize frustration by learning why we do the things we do. Over time, frustration grows to appreciation for God's creativity in designing personality.

How can you use your personality for God? First, learn about yourself. Pay attention to your mental habits, preferences, and patterns. You'll develop a better understanding on how and where to best serve. Your personality is one way God creates a unique place only you can fill. Second, learn about others. By understanding others you're better able to create united and harmonious relationships. "Can't they change to be more like me?" you ask. Oh, now wouldn't that be convenient. But also immeasurably boring! Contrary to what you may think, God didn't make people different just to drive you crazy. Our differences make us dynamic. When we work together using different gifts, diverse personalities, varied experiences and unique passions, we can be more like Christ. Variety adds spice to life. Spice adds flavor. Flavor is what makes life palatable. It makes life fun and serving interesting!

POINT TO PONDER

Understanding how your personality is wired helps you serve well in God's kingdom.

VERSE TO REMEMBER

"I will praise You, for I am fearfully and wonderfully made; Marvelous are Your works, And that my soul knows very well."

Psalm 139:14 (NKJV)

QUESTIONS TO CONSIDER

Do people who behave differently frustrate you or do you appreciate their differences? Why?

* Song written and performed by Nichole Nordeman
   Record Title: <u>This Mystery</u>
   Song Title: <u>Tremble</u>

Copyright 2000 Ariose Music

WEEK FOUR

NOTES

ABOUT FACE

Next to Jesus, the Apostle Paul is the most famous figure in the New Testament. Some have even called him the "second founder" of Christianity. History records that Paul was beheaded in Rome by the decree of the Roman emperor Nero. Paul's influence and memory is captured by the story surrounding his execution. Tradition claims that as Paul's

"But whatever things were gain to me, those things I have counted as loss for the sake of Christ."

Philippians 3:7 (NASB)

official sentence was being read, some daring person in the audience asserted, "The day will come when Christians will name their sons Paul and their dogs Nero."

WEEK FOUR

145

Paul's original Hebrew name was Saul. He was a Jewish man from Tarsus (Acts 22:3) with an impressive resume: "circumcised on the eighth day, of the people of Israel, of the tribe of Benjamin, a Hebrew of Hebrews; in regard to the law, a Pharisee; as for zeal, persecuting the church; as for legalistic righteousness, faultless" (Philippians 3:5-6, NIV). Religiously, Paul had cause for great confidence in himself and in his heritage. He continues, "But whatever was to my profit I now consider loss for the sake of Christ" (Philippians 3:7, NIV).

"Paul was an aggressive and zealous person long before becoming a follower of Jesus."

Jesus Christ had become Paul's all-consuming passion, even to the point of saying, "I have been crucified with Christ and I no longer live, but Christ lives in me. The life I live in the body, I live by faith in the Son of God, who loved me and gave himself for me" (Galatians 2:20, NIV). This wasn't always true in Paul's life. You see, Paul had a history. There was a time he wasn't living for Christ. He recounts some of his history in Galatians 1:11-24; grab a Bible and take a few minutes to read that passage right now.

Beginning in Galatians 1:11, Paul defends the charge that he was a false apostle by arguing that the Gospel he preached wasn't learned from anyone, but received directly from Jesus Christ. Paul then offers autobiographical information. Paul was an aggressive and zealous person long before becoming a follower of Jesus. He worked hard at destroying the Church of God. Zeal in a first century context quickly transformed to something you did with a knife. Paul, along with many of his contemporary Jews, longed for freedom from Roman oppression; this often equaled violence. Paul carried his zeal for the traditions of his ancestors to the extreme.

This aggression was leveled at the early church in Jerusalem as Saul stood and watched Stephen (the first Christian martyr) killed as "...the witnesses laid their clothes at the feet of a young man named Saul" (Acts 7:58b, NIV). The book of Acts continues to narrate Saul's attack, "But Saul began to destroy the church. Going from house to house, he dragged off men and women and put them in prison" (Acts 8:3, NIV). Finally, with authoritative letters from the Jewish high priest, Saul journeyed to Damascus intending to bring followers of this new "Way" back to Jerusalem for punishment. It is here where life changes for Saul. Acts 9:1-22 records the conversion and call of Paul the Apostle. Turn to this story and read this text at the end of this devotion.

As a zealous persecutor of the church, Paul sought to destroy the early band of Jesus' disciples. Now he himself had become a disciple of Jesus. God called Paul and set him apart by His grace for a specific purpose. It was time for Paul to "about face." God was redirecting him from zealous persecutor to zealous proclaimer of the Gospel of Christ. God specifically chose to use Paul's background, his passion and his gifts to serve *for* Christ, not against Him. When you read and study the Bible you can't help but become acquainted with Paul. He wrote thirteen of the New Testament documents consisting of letters to the many churches he founded and established as he traveled the Greco-Roman world preaching the Gospel of Jesus Christ.

WEEK FOUR

God wants to use your background, personality and gifts just as He used Paul's. You might say, "He could never use me because of... (whatever reason you might insert)." But listen to Paul. "Here is a trustworthy saying that deserves full acceptance: Christ Jesus came into the world to save sinners—of whom I am the worst. But for that very reason I was shown mercy so that in me, the worst of sinners, Christ Jesus might display his unlimited patience as an example for those who would believe in him and receive eternal life" (1 Timothy 1:15-16, NIV).

God will use your personality, your gifts and your experiences to further His kingdom both *in* you and *through* you. Like Paul, we must be willing to count our present pursuits, desires and goals as secondary to knowing Jesus. With Paul we must, "...want to know Christ and the power of his resurrection and the fellowship of sharing in his sufferings, becoming like him in his death" (Philippians 3:10, NIV). God used a zealous persecutor of the church in a dramatic way. As you surrender yourself to Him, He'll use you in ways beyond your wildest imagination. Just read Acts 9:1-22 and see what He did with Paul.

POINT TO PONDER

God will use your personality and abilities to serve in His kingdom.

VERSE TO REMEMBER

"But whatever things were gain to me, those things I have counted as loss for the sake of Christ." Philippians 3:7 (NASB)

QUESTION TO CONSIDER

What area(s) of your life do you need to surrender to Christ's authority?

NOTES

D A Y 24

CHARACTER VS. PERSONALITY

Have you ever noticed how someone's personality dictates his or her character? Many use their personality as an excuse for the things they do. They might say, "Oh, that's just how I am." For Christ-followers, that's *not* just how we are. Christ calls us to a life of selfless obedience. He set the standard. Our character should be reflected through our personality.

"Do not conform any longer to the pattern of this world, but be transformed by the renewing of your mind. Then you will be able to test and approve what God's will is—his good, pleasing and perfect will."
Romans 12:2 (NIV)

Peter learned the hard way. John 18:15-29 and 21:15-23 relates the

WEEK FOUR

story. Picture the scene. In the dark of night Jesus is arrested. Peter has just chopped off the ear of a Roman guard. As the entourage of soldiers takes away the shackled Savior, Peter cowardly follows in the distance peeking his head around corners and over fences to catch a glimpse. Jesus is taken into the chambers of Annas, the high priest, for trial. Scared and curious, Peter lingers in the courtyard shadows waiting to see what will happen next. A young lady approaches him saying, "Hey, didn't I see you with Jesus?" With his heart racing in fear he replies, "I don't know what you're talking about." Again he's approached and asked, "You look familiar. Didn't you come here with Jesus?" Now edgy, he blurts, "I don't know him." Wanting to run and hide, Peter makes his way outside the courtyard gates and is recognized by a group of men. One pipes up, "Your accent gives you away. You're not from here are you? Are you running around with Jesus?" Frustrated, Peter blows up. Matthew's account says Peter calls down curses on himself and denies knowing Jesus once again. Then Peter "went outside and wept bitterly" (Matthew 26:74-75, NIV).

Your depth of character manifests itself through your actions. Like Peter, do you ever walk away with a weeping heart? In this verse, the words used for weeping bitterly are related to deep grief, like the pain of losing a loved one. There's only one way to say it. Peter is a broken man, not only from *what* he's done, but also from *who* he's been. Ashamedly, at times I too find myself leaning back into my old way of life due to fear or insecurity.

Character is doing what's right, no matter what. As believers, we sometimes cave under pressure thinking about the outcome. Your kids or spouse might get angry. It wouldn't look good to the boss. Your co-workers might talk about you. Peter learned none of that mattered anymore. The shame in saving face was greater than taking the immediate heat.

The Bible offers advice for growing in this area of life. We must live under the authority of God's Word and let His power come alive in our hearts. Romans 12:2 (NIV) says, "Do not conform to the patterns of this world, but be transformed by the renewing of your mind. Then you will be able to test and approve what God's will is–his good, pleasing and perfect will." The word '*transform*' indicates something must take place inside of us; a change in focus of our heart and a deeper desire for obedience. '*Transform*' is also used to describe how Jesus was transfigured on a mountain in front of several disciples. Amazed, they

"Character at its most basic level is doing what's right, no matter what."

said, "His face shone like the sun and His clothes became as white as the light" (Matthew 17:2b, NIV).

When true transformation happens, you're different! You no longer look, think or walk the same way. God doesn't want us to remain the same. He longs to take us on a journey of change that remolds our character, thoughts and decisions. For most of us, like Peter, this change is a process.

Peter went into hiding after denying Christ. After rising from the dead, Jesus forgives Peter (John 21:15-19) and you see a changed man. He went from a man who allowed his personality flaws to get him rep-

rimanded by Jesus to a man who was humbled by the grace of Christ. A character transformation took place that surfaces later in Peter's life.

In Acts, Peter is now standing up for what is right, regardless of the personal cost:

- In Chapter 2 he boldly preaches to a Jewish crowd and 3000 come to Christ.
- In Chapter 3 he heals a man and preaches again.
- In Chapter 4 he is thrown in prison and put on trial for standing up for Christ.
- In Chapter 10 he teaches fellow Jews that God accepts all sects of people. This is hard for the Jews to hear.
- In Chapter 12 he escapes from prison after being tortured for preaching.

The list could go on. Yes, many people allow their personality to dictate their character. But God's heart and desire is that our character would dictate our personality. Doing what's right, no matter what, over-shadows personality flaws. Pray today that your character be immersed in the power of God's Word and that it would be apparent in the way you live.

POINT TO PONDER

God's heart and desire is that our character would dictate our personality.

VERSE TO REMEMBER

"Do not conform any longer to the pattern of this world, but be trans-formed by the renewing of your mind. Then you will be able to test and approve what God's will is-his good, pleasing and perfect will."
Romans 12:2 (NIV)

QUESTION TO CONSIDER

Are you allowing your personality to dictate your behavior or does your character dictate your personality?

WEEK FOUR

NOTES

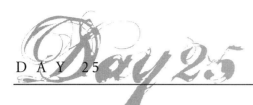

A LIFE
SO
LIVED

By now it should be clear. You were born for *something*. DNA research confirms that we're uniquely imprinted and wired from conception. Someday, we might be able to predict our God-given personality before it's evident. Amazing!

> *"...think of yourself with sober judgment,*
> *in accordance with the measure of faith God*
> *has given you."*
>
> Romans 12:3b (NIV)

The Bible is full of people doing what they were born to do. In studying these characters, the message is unmistakable. A personality turned over to God, redeemed for His purpose is a powerful thing—powerful enough to change the world and the course of history.

WEEK FOUR

Consider the story of Barnabas in the book of Acts. The profound effect of Barnabas' personality is captured in three distinct scenes. In Acts 4:36 (NIV), "Joseph, a Levite from Cyprus, whom the apostles called Barnabas (which means Son of Encouragement), sold a field he owned and brought the money and put it at the apostles' feet."

Barnabas was a member of the Levite tribe, or priestly Jews. He'd been exiled from his homeland and grew up on the Island of Cyprus. He likely spoke a different language, a point of contention for many Jerusalem natives. He'd lost his priestly rights his entire life and was now home where he should've finally enjoyed a priestly status.

Still, there was no hostility or resentment in Barnabas, but rather, a wonderful self-forgetfulness that only becomes more evident as his story continues. Barnabas saw his early Christian brothers in need and simply responded by selling what was rightfully his and selflessly laying it at the feet of the Apostles. *He turned it over to God with no strings attached.*

> "Barnabas' personality couldn't be used by God if he hadn't at some point looked in the mirror and realized who God made him to be and humbly turned over his personality for God's glory."

Our second scene takes place in Acts 9:26, 27 (NIV).
"When he (Paul) came to Jerusalem, he tried to join the disciples, but they were all afraid of him, not believing that he really was a disciple.

But Barnabas took him and brought him to the apostles. He told them
how Saul on his journey had seen the Lord and that the Lord had spoken
to him, and how in Damascus he had preached fearlessly in the name of
Jesus."

After his profound conversion experience on the road to Damascus
that we discussed a few days ago, the once murderous Paul is coming to
serve the church he'd persecuted. The church in Jerusalem is SO aware
that Paul is a dangerous dude that they want nothing to do with him.
They aren't willing to think about it, hear his thoughts or even look him
in the eye. Can you picture a not-so-holy team huddle trying to figure
out who'll hang out with Paul?

"I'm not doing it!"

"Me either."

"I don't trust that guy."

"I don't blame you."

"Let's get Barnabas to do it. He likes everyone."

This selfless lover and encourager of people puts his arm around the
reviled Paul and by doing so, unleashes one of the greatest ministers the
church has ever known. Paul would later spread the Gospel to the rest of
the world, plant multiple churches and write much of our God-inspired
New Testament. In that moment, *Barnabas' redeemed personality probably
changed the world*.

Our final scene is in Acts 11:20-23 (NIV), "Some of them, however,
men from Cyprus and Cyrene, went to Antioch and began to speak to
Greeks also, telling them the good news about the Lord Jesus...News of
this reached the ears of the church at Jerusalem, and they sent Barnabas

WEEK FOUR

to Antioch. When he arrived and saw the evidence of the grace of God, he was glad and encouraged them all to remain true to the Lord with all their hearts."

During the first decade of the church, the Gospel of Christ was primarily a Jewish thing. Christianity was thought of as a sect of Judaism. To Jewish Christians, to be a Christian was to be a Jew. When the Gospel began spreading outside Judaism into the Gentile world it was a profoundly new day. A day rejected by most Jewish Christians.

But Barnabas saw the Gospel as Christ intended it—as good news for *all*. He was the first Jewish church leader who welcomed Gentiles into the Christian faith. Later he defended non-Jewish Christianity. I'm so grateful he did! Again, *a man's redeemed personality not only changed THE world, it changed MY world.*

Barnabas' story is rich with lessons on encouragement for using your spiritual gifts and your personality for God's glory. But as powerful as it is, Barnabas' personality couldn't be used by God if he hadn't at some point looked in the mirror, realized who God made him to be and humbly handed over his personality for God's glory.

Do you spend time trying to be something you're not? Are you trying to please people or God? I wonder if there was a poignant moment in Barnabas' life as he realized God had "wonderfully knit him together" and he was "God's workmanship." Maybe a conscious moment when he died to being something *he wanted* to be and realized what *God made* him to be. The power of a life so lived is undeniable.

Take a look in the mirror. Be honest. Be intentional. Figure out your wiring and let God's power flow through it. God only knows what can happen. He really does. Maybe you'll get a glimpse of it too when you read the story of Barnabas.

POINT TO PONDER

Your personality is a part of your DNA.

VERSE TO REMEMBER

"...think of yourself with sober judgment, in accordance with the measure of faith God has given you." Romans 12:3b (NIV)

QUESTIONS TO CONSIDER

What specific personality strengths and weaknesses do you see in yourself? Are you willing to be what God made you to be and let your God-given personality be used for His glory?

WEEK FOUR

NOTES

BLESSED
TO GIVE

What kinds of people serve God best? What character traits does God look for in choosing people for His team? If you took a survey, you'd probably get answers related to intelligence, righteousness, patience, tolerance, even temperament, humility, few character flaws and clean lifestyle. That's quite a list! Could any of us live up to it?

"All peoples on earth will be blessed
through you and your offspring. I
am with you and will watch over
you wherever you go."
Genesis 28:14b-15a (NIV)

Fortunately, we don't have to guess or rely on a survey to see the kinds of people God works through. The answers are recorded in the

WEEK FOUR

163

Bible. All through the Bible, we witness God's work firsthand through imperfect, everyday people like us: people who lie, doubt, and make mistakes but don't learn from them, people who live the consequences of previous actions and choices, people who try to cope with dysfunctional families and people who are short-tempered or impetuous. The Bible also shows God working through people who are afraid, tired or grieving. He even worked through adulterers, liars and murderers.

Today we'll see how God enlisted a lying cheater named Jacob to do His work. You'll find his story in Genesis, chapters 25 – 35. I encourage you to read through it this week. You'll be intrigued by Jacob's continual attempt to cheat his way through life and keep his dysfunctional family in balance, all the while being chosen by God to bless others.

Jacob was born trying to get ahead. He came out of the womb grabbing his twin brother Esau's heel, trying to be the firstborn. (In those days, the firstborn received the majority of the inheritance.) As the boys grew up, Jacob deceived his brother into signing over his firstborn rights. He then lied to his ailing, elderly father and pretended to be Esau so he would receive the family blessing.

Jacob thought he had to be someone else in order to receive God's blessing.

Can you relate to Jacob? We assume since God knows everything about us, He'd never use us for His work. Surely God would rather enlist someone else. We assume this because we compare what we *know* about ourselves to what we *don't know* about others. Then we decide that other people have their lives more together than we do.

God wants to hand you His blessing regardless of your personality flaws. Now understand, the Bible neither condones nor ignores such flaws. It even warns people who continue to make poor choices or who find themselves damaging others because of their shortcomings. Galatians 6: 7 (NIV) says, "Do not be deceived: God cannot be mocked. A man reaps what he sows."

Our personality flaws certainly get us into trouble, sometimes with devastating consequences. In part, God's commands are to protect us from what happens when we live on our own terms. Even though Jacob received God's blessing, he still suffered the consequences of his shortcomings. His continual practice of deceit earned him a death threat from his brother, estrangement from his in-laws and continual strife between the four mothers of his children, including his two wives.

But as Jacob's story clearly teaches, God's blessing is not negated by our

> "God's blessing is not negated by our shortcomings."

shortcomings. Even after Jacob deceived his brother and father, Genesis 28:14b-15 (NIV) records God coming to Jacob saying, "All peoples on earth will be blessed through you and your offspring. I am with you and will watch over you wherever you go, and I will bring you back to this land. I will not leave you until I have done what I have promised you."

God's blessing to Jacob carried two promises: Jacob would be God's representative to unsaved people, and God would always be with Jacob. God brings us blessings not to hold tight and keep, but to share with others.

WEEK FOUR

What blessings has God given you that you can use to help others? They may be material things, talents, skills or financial blessings. In keeping with Jacob's example, maybe God has given you something to share with an un-churched person. God gives His blessing that we may bless others. His blessing is a gift. We can't take credit for it.

Jacob's personality flaws didn't disqualify or excuse him from being used by God. As online pastor Wade Hodges says, "I may not like Jacob, but I love the story of how God uses him. Jacob's life takes away our excuses for running away from God."

God won't bless me, I don't deserve it.
God won't use me, I'm not reliable.
God could never love me, I'm not good enough.*

The Hebrew word for these kinds of excuses is "hogwash."

POINT TO PONDER

Personality flaws don't disqualify or excuse you from receiving God's blessing.

VERSE TO REMEMBER

"All peoples on earth will be blessed through you and your offspring. I am with you and will watch over you wherever you go."
Genesis 28:14b-15a (NIV)

QUESTION TO CONSIDER

God's blessings are given so you can give to others. What has He given you that you can share with others?

*http://www.wadehodges.com/Audio/genesis/jacob.htm)

WEEK FOUR

NOTES

TYPECASTING

God created each person as a unique masterpiece, but personality differences are not random. Our characteristics are identifiable and often predictable. We approach situations with a set of automatic responses and act in ways we're most comfortable. A responsible, hardworking person will rarely deviate from that style regardless of the situation. A

"If it is possible, as far as it depends on you, live at peace with everyone."
Romans 12:18 (NIV)

perpetually lighthearted person is generally more carefree and easygoing than our more serious example. Behavior is a natural manifestation of your inborn personality. And as we've seen this week, God can use all kinds of personalities.

WEEK FOUR

Personality can be divided into four major areas. These areas help us recognize and identify our natural strengths and potential weaknesses. Understanding how we're alike and how we're different helps us to value and even celebrate our differences. Over the next two days, we'll look at a broad description of the psychological instrument called the Myers-Briggs Type Indicator, MBTI®. It's routinely used in business to help motivate, problem solve, manage conflicts, build teams, enhance communication and help individuals learn where they best fit in, be it at work or in their relationships. It can also be used to help you discover where to best serve in God's kingdom.

According to the Meyers-Briggs Type Indicator®, there are four components that make up a personality type. They are:

1. How you are energized: Extravert (E) or Introvert (I),
2. The kind of information you naturally notice and remember: Sensing (S) or Intuition (N),
3. How you make decisions: Thinking (T) or Feeling (F),
4. How you organize your world: Judging (J) or Perceiving (P).

Each of these dimensions deals with an important aspect of life and provides accurate insights into our own behavior and the behavior of others. Each person has one of each dimension, making a four-letter combination, such as ISTJ or ENFP. There are 16 types in all. Everyone will naturally and easily fit into one of them.

You may use both sides of one dimension, but no one uses them with equal frequency, energy or success. Have you ever tried to eat or write with your non-dominant hand? It's clumsy, but you can do it. You also have a preference in personality traits. It's not that you can't use your less preferred trait; it's just not as comfortable. You'll naturally choose what takes less time or energy and what's more productive for you. Everyone is primarily one way or the other but not exclusively that way.

Today we'll look at the first two dimensions described above. Extravert or Introvert is about your energy. Where do you get it and where do you direct it? Are you energized most by interacting with other people or being by yourself? Do you enjoy focusing your energy in the outer world of people and things or in the inner world of ideas and thoughts? Extraverts are "other-centered." They get energy from and focus their energy toward people and things outside of themselves. The more interactions with others, the more energized they are. Introverts are more "self-centered." This doesn't mean selfish, but rather self-contained and self-reliant. Introverts are more thoughtful, contemplative and deliberate. They're content to be alone or with one other person for an extended length of time.

Extraverts generally have many friends and acquaintances while Introverts prefer a few close friends. Extraverts often need to talk in order to think. Introverts will think before they talk. Extraverts work rapidly, driven by action. Introverts prefer working slowly and carefully. Introverts prefer to immerse themselves in a project that interests them. They're naturally independent and find the solitude of working alone stimulating and refreshing. Extraverts notoriously find excuses for not focusing on one thing. They're much more interested in and energized by their external environment.

WEEK FOUR

The second type dimension describes how people perceive information. The Sensor takes in information primarily through the five senses— what they see, hear, touch, taste or smell. The Intuitive takes in information through a sixth sense, focusing not on what is, but on what could be. Do you pay more attention to facts and details or try to understand connections, underlying meaning and implications? Are you down-to-earth and sensible or imaginative and creative? Do you trust your direct experience or your gut instinct? Do you live for the moment or imagine how things will affect future events?

Sensing and Intuition represent the greatest differences between people since they influence worldview. Sensors think in a linear fashion, one thought following the next. Intuitives engage in spontaneous leaps in thinking. Sensors respond to the practical, functional, useful and real. Intuitives crave inspiration and are bored with routine. Their energy flows wherever inspiration lies. Intuitives express

"Understanding how we're alike and how we're different helps us to value and even celebrate our differences."

creativity in seeing or doing things differently than before. Sensors demonstrate creativity by finding a new application for something already invented or established. Intuitives are the "thinker-uppers" and Sensors are the "getter-doners." Sensors must engage their senses in the mastery of practical skills and Intuitive types must follow whatever inspires.

Learning more about what drives your personality and motivates others provides incredible insight into yourself and those around you.

It'll help you discover how you can best serve God by serving others, ultimately advancing His kingdom on earth. Tomorrow we'll look at the last two dimensions in personality type and get a glimpse of how all four dimensions work together. It's an exciting journey into how God wired you as an individual and as part of His dynamic family.

POINT TO PONDER
Behavior is a natural manifestation of your inborn personality.

VERSE TO REMEMBER
"If it is possible, as far as it depends on you, live at peace with everyone."
Romans 12:18 (NIV)

QUESTIONS TO CONSIDER
Of the first two dimensions discussed today, where do you fit in? Do you have more Introvert or Extravert characteristics? Do you tend to perceive things as a Sensor or an Intuitive? What about those closest to you?

WEEK FOUR

NOTES

TAILOR-MADE

"...that you may be filled with the knowledge of His will in all wisdom and spiritual understanding; that you may walk worthy of the Lord, fully pleasing Him, being fruitful in every good work and increasing in the knowledge of God; strengthened with all might, according to His glorious power, for all patience and longsuffering with joy; giving thanks to the Father who has qualified us to be partakers of the inheritance of the saints in the light."

Colossians 1:9-12 (NKJV)

WEEK FOUR

Isn't God amazing? The more I learn about our intricate world and the incredible inner workings of our bodies, the more in awe I am of our wonderful Creator. Personality is just one of the many ways that God made you, uniquely you. Your personality is a complex tool for serving Him. Yesterday, we began our brief study by looking at the first two dimensions in type—Extravert or Introvert and Sensor or Intuitive. Today we'll explore the final two dimensions and take a look at how all four work together.

While Sensing and Intuition describe how we take in information, Thinking and Feeling describe how we make decisions or come to conclusions. Both Thinking and Feeling describe rational decision-making processes; Thinkers have feelings and Feelers are capable of logic. Do you weigh the pros and cons or consider how others will be affected by your decision? Is it more important to be truthful or tactful? Would you rather be tough or tender?

Logic rules for thinkers. They analyze the issue logically and impersonally, asking if it makes sense. Feelers personalize the situation and imagine how others would feel about it. Thinkers need to be right. Feelers need to be liked. Thinkers don't mean to be cruel, any more than Feelers mean to be dishonest. But Thinkers value truth and honesty while Feelers value tact and diplomacy. Thinkers claim they're tenderhearted and Feelers can be surprisingly unyielding in their personal convictions. Thinkers must pursue logical order. Feelers must follow their hearts.

The final type dimension—Perceivers and Judgers—describes how we organize our world. The Perceiver has an innate drive to keep things open, and continue taking in information. Judgers have the opposite

drive—to close things down and make a decision. Do you plan or wing it? Do you like things settled or to leave your options open? Do you like controlling a situation or to let others call the shots? Are you punctual or are you frequently late? Are you organized or impulsive? Do you have files or piles? Do you work before play or play while you work?

The Judger feels better with a decision made. The Perceiver likes to keep options open. Judgers have strong opinions on everything and share them. Perceivers can have strong opinions but see shades of gray rather than the Judger's black and white. Perceivers see both sides of an issue. They're spontaneous and shift gears quickly. They procrastinate and don't take themselves too seriously. Judgers are decisive, organized and productive. They fulfill their obligations, reach their goals and are on time. Judgers follow the rules. Perceivers question rules and break them sometimes just for the fun of it.

"Personality is just one of the many ways that God made you, uniquely you. Your personality is a complex tool for serving Him."

As you can see, we've only scratched the surface. I hope this little tour has given you a better understanding of yourself and those around you. When you start looking at the combinations of these dimensions you can see how the total is greater than the sum of the parts. None of the dimensions operate in isolation. People who are ISTJ and people who are INFP may share the Introvert dimension but are very different

WEEK FOUR

personalities as all others letters are opposite. Even a one-letter difference can be profound.

Personality is just one of the many aspects in how God uniquely wired you. When you combine your personality with your passions, spiritual gifts, experiences and abilities your true shape comes to life. You begin to see how your ideal place of service is truly tailor-made especially for you by the Creator Himself. And that, my friend, is absolutely awesome!

POINT TO PONDER

Your personality is a complex tool for serving God.

VERSE TO REMEMBER

"…that you may be filled with the knowledge of His will in all wisdom and spiritual understanding; that you may walk worthy of the Lord fully pleasing Him, being fruitful in every good work and increasing in the knowledge of God; strengthened with all might, according to His glorious power, for all patience and longsuffering with joy; giving thanks to the Father who has qualified us to be partakers of the inheritance of the saints in the light." Colossians 1:9-12 (NKJV)

QUESTIONS TO CONSIDER

What is your type-dimension combination? How can you best use it to serve God and others?

NOTES

....

....

....

....

....

....

....

....

....

....

....

....

....

....

....

....

....

....

....

....

....

....

* From *People Types & Tiger Stripes*, 1993, by Gordon D. Lawrence. Used
  with permission.
  Center for Applications of Psychological Type, Gainesville, FL • www.capt.org

WEEK FOUR

WEEK 5

SURRENDERING YOUR PAST

"You intended to harm me, but God intended it for good to accomplish what is now being done, the saving of many lives."

Genesis 50:20 (NIV)

LIFE'S COLD SHOWERS

God's been preparing you since before you were born. He's preparing you to live a life pleasing to Him. It can be a struggle to stay focused on God in daily life. It's hard to deny the tendencies pulling us away from

"Consider it pure joy, my brothers, whenever you face trials of many kinds, because you know that the testing of your faith develops perseverance. Perseverance must finish its work so that you may become mature and complete, not lacking anything."

James 1:2-4 (NIV)

God. Paul wrote, "I have been crucified with Christ; it is no longer I who live, but Christ lives in me; and the life which I now live in the flesh I live

WEEK FIVE

by faith in the Son of God, who loved me and gave Himself for me" (Galatians 2:20, NASB). Paul talks about dying to ourselves and allowing Christ to live through us. As we saw a few days ago, he later encourages the church in Rome, "do not be conformed to this world, but be transformed by the renewing of your mind, that you may prove what the will of God is, that which is good and acceptable and perfect" (Romans 12:2, NASB).

Paul knew it was a struggle to live a life set apart from the world. He lived in a time just as evil, corrupt and self-serving as we do. His words still ring true to Christians today; flush out the bad and focus on the good things God does in your life. Continually renew and recharge your batteries on the free power that comes only from God.

"Every bad experience we have on earth is inconsequential compared to the glory we'll experience in heaven."

When I was in college, I went to Panama on my first mission trip. My friends had been on mission trips and talked excitedly about their life-changing experiences. I looked forward to what God would teach me with earnest expectation. The trip was incredible, but the most memorable times were also the most miserable: the morning showers.

We were guests in a home with no hot water. Morning showers were painfully cold. I can still vividly remember the icy cold water pounding my bare back and the feeling of my feet on the frigid concrete floor those chilly mornings. It was so miserable I almost regretted going on the trip. I endured those showers only on the hope and understanding that soon (not soon enough) I'd be at home in the States, taking the longest, hottest shower ever known to man.

On the plane ride home, our trip leader asked each of us to write a brief summary of our mission experience. Sitting there on the plane, I felt gypped. I hadn't had a life-changing experience. I was disappointed. I wanted my money back. How foolish I was indeed!

Once at home, I cranked up the heat and took the longest shower my little water heater could provide. During that shower I recalled the freezing ones I took in Panama and wondered how I tolerated them. Then I knew. It was the hope. I had held onto the hope and knowledge that I was just passing through. It was a temporary situation. And while a hot shower is trivial in the grand scheme of things, the *hope* was key.

We have the hope and knowledge that we're just travelers passing through. This life on earth is a temporary situation. One day you and I will be with Jesus in heaven and every bad experience we have on earth will be inconsequential compared to the glory we'll experience in heaven. Paul said, "For I consider that the sufferings of this present time are not worthy to be compared with the glory that is to be revealed to us" (Romans 8:18, NASB). Paul figured it out. This life is temporary. Nothing we experience will overshadow the glory of being united with God in heaven.

We all have unique experiences in life. You may think your life experiences are meaningless, but not so in God's mind. They're unique, incredible opportunities to learn more about yourself and His plans for

WEEK FIVE

your future. He's been preparing you to learn from each of your experiences and to share them with others. Each is a new stepping-stone to the next season in life.

Next time you go through a difficult time, remember the words of James: "Consider it pure joy, my brothers, whenever you face trials of many kinds, because you know that the testing of your faith develops perseverance. Perseverance must finish its work so that you may become mature and complete, not lacking anything" (James 1:2-4, NIV). God wants to make you complete in Him. What about your life experiences? Which can He use to minister to others? Allow God to teach you through experiences and share them with others who need encouragement.

POINT TO PONDER

Your life experiences are opportunities to minister to others.

VERSE TO REMEMBER

"Consider it pure joy, my brothers, whenever you face trials of many kinds, because you know that the testing of your faith develops perseverance. Perseverance must finish its work so that you may become mature and complete, not lacking anything." James 1:2-4 (NIV)

QUESTIONS TO CONSIDER

In what ways or areas have you had to persevere in life? How can you use those experiences to benefit and minister to others?

NOTES

PLOT TWISTS & SURPRISE ENDINGS

I love reading books and watching movies with surprise endings and unexpected plot twists. One of my favorites is the movie, *The Sixth Sense*. In it, Bruce Willis plays a psychologist trying to help a boy who claims to see dead people. The writer cleverly and expertly disguises the truth.

"You intended to harm me, but God intended it for good."

Genesis 50:20 (NIV)

With a surprise twist we realize the psychologist is actually dead himself. Neither he nor the audience had realized it. Ultimately, it's the little boy who helps him. The closing scene flashes back to all the hints along the way revealing that Willis' character never interacts with any of the living characters except for the little boy who in fact, *does* see dead people. In hindsight, the conclusion is obvious. But the unfolding story keeps you so engrossed you miss the obvious along the way.

Life is often like that. Things are running along so smoothly you presume to know what tomorrow will bring. Your relationships are great, work is motivating and the kids are healthy. Then the phone rings and you learn there's been an accident. The boss says the company is downsizing. The doctor explains that it's malignant. Your spouse is in love with your best friend. A letter arrives from the IRS. Suddenly life has an unwelcome and surprising plot twist. You never saw it coming.

As Christ-followers, we sometimes think we're immune to plot twists. Isn't God the author of our lives? Doesn't He work all things together for the good? For a better answer, let's look at the story of Joseph. (You can follow along by reading Genesis 37:1 – 50:20.)

Joseph had everything going for him. He was young, good-looking, wealthy and his father's favorite child. Although he was the second youngest of twelve sons, he was the heir apparent to his father's ranching empire. He knew this was his divine destiny because God spoke to him through dreams where he saw his brothers bowing down to him. But his brothers had a different future in mind. They planned to turn young Joseph's dream into a nightmare by plotting to kill him and blaming his death on wild animals. They later decided to make some money and sell Joseph to some slave traders passing by. Joseph's dream had its first sudden and unexpected plot twist.

Joseph was sold to Potiphar, a high official in the Egyptian royal court. Scripture says the Lord was with Joseph and blessed him. Potiphar

WEEK FIVE

recognized the Lord's blessing on Joseph and trusted him with his household and business affairs. So Joseph rose to the top, second only to Potiphar.

Things were going better than expected until the second plot twist. The Bible says Joseph was "well-built" and "handsome," and that Potiphar's wife was lonely and neglected. She made Joseph an offer she thought too good to refuse saying, "Come to bed with me." Joseph declined, not wanting to sin against Potiphar or God. But everyday she repeated her request. Frustrated by rejection, she accused Joseph of rape. Potiphar hated losing a trusted servant, but his honor was at stake and after all, Joseph was only a slave. So because of his integrity and for doing the right and godly thing, Joseph earned a spot in the royal prison.

Still, God honored Joseph's integrity and blessed him. The warden grew to trust Joseph and put him in charge of the other prisoners. He was second only to the warden. While in prison, God helped Joseph interpret the dreams of two royal prisoners. One of them, Pharaoh's cupbearer, was freed. Gratefully, he promised to put in a good word for Joseph, but then promptly forgot.

Two years went by. Then one night Pharaoh had a dream nobody could interpret. The cupbearer remembered how Joseph had interpreted his dream and told Pharaoh. Joseph was called out of prison and through God's intervention, explained Pharaoh's dream as a warning of coming prosperity to be followed by famine. Impressed, Pharaoh put Joseph in charge of all of Egypt. Now Joseph was second only to Pharaoh. Eventually, Joseph's brothers traveled to Egypt and bowed down to Joseph in their quest for food. This is how, through unexpected plot twists and

surprise endings; Joseph's divine dream finally came true.

A great piece of biblical wisdom comes from the confrontation between Joseph and his brothers at the end of this story. In a single phrase, Joseph sums up his life and forgives his brothers saying, "You intended to harm me, but God intended it for good" (Genesis 50:20, NIV). Only God could orchestrate the twists and turns of Joseph's life. And only in hindsight do we see God's hand in it. Joseph's commitment to serve God through every challenge and hardship put him in a position to save his family from starvation and to realize the destiny God had dreamed for him.

"As Christ-followers, we sometimes think we're immune to plot twists."

So what about the plot twists and surprises in your life? Are you complaining and wondering where God is? Or are you striving to see God's hand in every aspect of your life, knowing He uses every situation, challenge and hardship for your good, for His good and for the good of others.

WEEK FIVE

POINT TO PONDER

The very thing that presses so hard against you is the perfect tool, in the hand of the Master, to shape you for eternity. So don't resist and push it away, lest you spoil His work.

VERSE TO REMEMBER

"As far as I am concerned, God turned into good what you meant for evil. He brought me to the high position I have today so I could save the lives of many people." Genesis 50:20 (NLT)

QUESTIONS TO CONSIDER

In what ways has your life taken some unexpected turns or plot twists? What did you learn from those experiences? How can you use them to minister to others?

NOTES

D A Y 31

LIFE
STINKS

Sometimes life stinks. Everyday you arise to attack the day. But some days go every way but the way you intended. It's a bad hair day, your car won't start and sibling rivalry is at an all-time high in your household. Still, all that is trivial when something serious happens something that tries every ounce of your faith: your mother dies, your spouse is seriously

"Praise be to the God and Father of our Lord Jesus Christ, the Father of compassion and the God of all comfort, who comforts us in all our troubles, so that we can comfort those in any trouble with the comfort we ourselves have received from God."

2 Corinthians 1:3-4 (NIV)

injured or your child goes wayward. Life-changing events are like rocks upsetting the tranquil pond of life. They can ripple through the hearts and lives of many as the lasting effects set in. Why does our all-powerful God let His children experience the darker sides of life?

Yesterday we looked at the life of Joseph and how he handled with grace the many plot twists and surprises he was dealt. The Bible says trials are beneficial to us. Matthew 5:4 (NIV) says, "Blessed are those who mourn, for they will be comforted." Life's trials and tribulations are not just something God *lets* us experience while He looks on idly. They're an integral part of growing in our spiritual lives.

Have you ever prayed that God would use you? Maybe you prayed big, wanting Him to use you in an important way at a worldwide level. Maybe you prayed small, wanting Him to use you to make a difference in little ways, helping people you pass in daily life. There's nothing wrong with praying like this. It's great when God's people rise to the challenge of serving. But we have a tendency to forget that in order to prepare us for His service, He may bring us through a time of training and seasoning.

This is where our expectations of God often go against our grain. We rarely wish to experience trials and hardships in preparing for kingdom service. But how valid is this frame of mind? Would you expect your doctor to forego the grueling hours of medical school? Would you feel comfortable flying with a pilot who went straight from high school to the cockpit? We get so excited for what God will have us do *in life* we forget about what God is going to do *in us* to enable His will to happen.

The most pivotal moments in life are often the most painful. It's

WEEK FIVE

the drug addiction you faced in your twenties when God was less than an afterthought. It's the years of recovery, support groups and medical ailments before finding God and praising Him with every fiber of your being. It's, lo and behold, helping an addiction-recovery group of young people. All the days and nights you cursed God, all the hardship and pain, are now making an impact on the lives of kids.

What about the abusive marriage you left behind? After debating with God and yourself, you finally took the advice of your pastor and counselor and filed for divorce. You spent five years mourning, growing and healing. Then one day you get a call. A leader is needed for a new support group for wives in abusive relationships. Can you help? Now your painful experiences are helping other women. In your eyes they see new hope and the life-giving grace from God.

"Life's trials and tribulations are not just something God *lets* us experience while He looks on idly. They're an integral part of growing in our spiritual lives."

Okay, so God uses our painful experiences to minister to others. But why does it only sound good after the fact? Does anyone ever desire to experience hurt and pain for the good of others? Of course not! Naturally we enjoy the good times in life. So how do we use the less desirable times for God when we don't want them in the first place? Here's some advice.

1. Accept that life isn't perfect. Every Christian has difficult times. John 16:33 (NIV) says, "I have told you these things, so that in me you may have peace. In this world you will have trouble. But take heart! I have overcome the world." Life is not without trouble. Jesus affirmed this. But thankfully He didn't just say, "Life's going to stink. See you when you get back home." No, instead He offered peace in walking with Him.

2. Thank God for the opportunity to experience a trial. No one wants to go through trials, but they refine us into the person God needs us to be, to do what He wants us to do. Thank God that you're right where you are in life right now—whether it's a difficult place, or an easy one.

3. Once you've recovered from your difficult time, look for opportunities to use it to serve others. 2 Corinthians 1:3-4 (NIV) says, "Praise be to the God and Father of our Lord Jesus Christ, the Father of compassion and the God of all comfort, who comforts us in all our troubles, so that we can comfort those in any trouble with the comfort we ourselves have received from God."

Just as Joseph discovered, the trials we face in life aren't useless. We can use our experiences to serve God in amazing ways.

WEEK FIVE

POINT TO PONDER

God uses your past to enrich other people's future.

VERSE TO REMEMBER

"Praise be to the God and Father of our Lord Jesus Christ, the Father of compassion and the God of all comfort, who comforts us in all our troubles, so that we can comfort those in any trouble with the comfort we ourselves have received from God." 2 Corinthians 1:3-4 (NIV)

QUESTIONS TO CONSIDER

What experiences in your past were hardships or painful? How did you grow from these experiences? How can you use them as opportunities to serve others?

NOTES

A MOTHER'S WORST NIGHTMARE

His curfew was 10:00 p.m. The 911 call came in at 9:53 p.m. By 10:00 p.m, he was home. But not the home his mother expected. For her, the news was bittersweet. Her sixteen-year-old son was in heaven with our Lord, but gone from her presence. He would never walk through the door of their home again.

> *"He comforts us in all our troubles so that we can comfort others. When others are troubled, we will be able to give them the same comfort God has given us."*
>
> 2 Corinthians 1:4 (NLT)

From that night forward, Jayne Post's life was different, but she refused to retreat into darkness. She read books about grieving, had lengthy discussions with God about her true feelings and dived into His Word. She learned to receive strength from God.

How does God comfort? In order to share God's comfort, we must first understand how He comforts us. When trouble surrounds us, He doesn't remove our hardship, but gives us strength to endure. He didn't bring Jayne's son back to life, but He gave her the strength to carry on, even when she felt weak and helpless.

"I learned there are worse things than death for a Christian because death is our only portal to heaven and to Jesus," Jayne shares. "I also learned to ask God where He's working and why, so I could know His purpose." Because of her son's death, many people have come to know Christ as their personal Savior. And for that reason alone, she feels her son would say it was worth dying for.

When does God comfort us? The Bible says God comforts us in all our troubles. (2 Corinthians 1:4) It doesn't say before, during or after our troubles, but IN our troubles. He's there at all times to strengthen and comfort us. It's easy to thank God when things are going well. But what about when things go wrong? We wonder where He is and how He could allow such terrible things to happen. It's difficult when things go wrong. We may not feel His presence during our troubles but He's there nonetheless.

Why does God comfort us? Paul writes, "...so that we can comfort others. When others are troubled, we will be able to give them the same comfort God has given us" (2 Corinthians 1:4, NLT). God wants us to comfort others in the same way He comforts us, by walking with them through their troubles. We can't remove the troubles of others, but we

WEEK FIVE

can offer strength through encouragement, hope and prayer.

When Jayne's son died, she experienced the pain of grief and loss no parent ever wants to bear. The loss will always be there. But so will the comfort that only God could provide. What she didn't know at the time was how soon she would be called upon to comfort others. Only months later, she would guide friends through the same journey of healing. One friend's mother died. Another friend suffered the death of her baby boy. The husband of yet another friend passed away. A fourth friend experienced the loss of her close friend. One by one, the calls came. It was only through Jayne's personal loss that she could offer comfort, sympathy and most of all, true empathy. Jayne constantly re-minds her friends that God cares and is with them. Jeremiah 42:11(KJV) says, "Be not afraid...saith the Lord: for I (am) with you to save you...and to deliver you."

"It was only through Jayne's personal loss that she could offer comfort, sympathy and most of all, true empathy."

As Christians, we understand that death leads to an everlasting life with Christ. That's cause for rejoicing! But it doesn't mean we don't feel loss and grief when we lose someone dear to us. Jayne comforts her friends in letting them know it's okay to cry and mourn over our loved ones. Jesus wept over the death of His friend Lazarus. She also encourag-es forgiveness because no matter what we do, God says, "I forgive you." He doesn't say, "I have to think about it" or "Maybe later." He immediately forgives us. Likewise, we have to do the same for those who hurt us. For Jayne, it was easy to forgive the sixteen-year-old boy responsible for her son's accident because of God's free and immediate forgiveness.

Jayne also says you can prepare yourself now for tough times ahead. How? Surround yourself with a community of close friends who strengthen you and will be there for you when you need them. Jayne says, "I couldn't have done this alone. My community of friends at church helped me survive."

God gives you strength to endure your trials. He is always there for you when you need Him. Like Jayne, you can serve others by sharing the comfort you've received from Him.

POINT TO PONDER
God comforts us in times of need so we can comfort others in kind, during their times of trouble.

VERSE TO REMEMBER
"He comforts us in all our troubles so that we can comfort others."
1 Corinthians 1:4a (NLT)

QUESTIONS TO CONSIDER
How can using your own painful and difficult times to help others in turn help you to heal? Are you willing to be open and honest about your pain and hardship to help yourself and others?

WEEK FIVE

DAY 32

NOTES

HARD KNOCK LIFE

"Experience is the hardest kind of teacher," someone said, "it gives you the test first and the lesson afterward." While there's truth to that, experience is the best teacher. Part of discovering our purpose involves reflecting on what we've gone through, and then reaching out to others going through similar struggles.

"God doesn't want us to be shy with his gifts, but bold and loving and sensible."
2 Timothy 1:7 (MSG)

God wants to use our family, educational and vocational backgrounds for His purposes. As we explore our life experiences, we discover more of who we are and how God can use us. Consider Moses, who grew up in Pharaoh's court in Egypt thousands of years ago. He was

raised as a prince of Egypt for 40 years. Egypt was the most cultured, educated, wealthy environment in the world. Imagine being raised a prince in the wealthiest nation on earth. "Moses was educated in all the learning of the Egyptians, and he was a man of power in words and deeds" (Acts 7:22, NASB).

But Moses was also a Hebrew. When he saw an Egyptian slave master beating a Hebrew slave, he grew angry and killed the slave master in a fit of rage. Fearing for his life, Moses fled to the desert. For 40 years he roamed the desert. His dreams faded. He felt like a failure. How could he go from the courts of Pharaoh to no man's land, from privilege to menial labor as a shepherd, from popularity to anonymity? Moses lived in the desert, but God had not deserted him.

We often speak of faith in terms of renewal, power and fulfillment; but rarely do we speak of the desert. The desert maintains a special place in spiritual formation. Without the desert, Moses would've been unprepared to lead. He needed the desert's lessons.

Moses was a senior citizen before God called him out of that desert to face the biggest challenge of his life—confronting Pharaoh and demanding he set the Israelite people free from slavery. His experience of living in Egypt and the desert were essential in fulfilling his purpose.

Think about your family life. What kinds of unique family experiences have you had? How could God use those experiences to help and encourage others? Consider your work and educational background. What have you learned over the years? How could you use that knowledge to fulfill God's purpose for your life? An auto mechanic could help repair cars for single moms. A contractor could leverage his experience

for the church. A graphic artist could lend her expertise to a ministry. An early childhood specialist could volunteer to help children.

Bill entered the Marine Corps right after high school. He rose through the ranks to become a colonel with some of the highest security clearances possible. Throughout his career he lived in more than forty countries and traveled to more than eighty. He left his blood on three continents due to battle and still carries shrapnel as a reminder. But all of that was preparation for God's greater purpose, which came *after* Bill retired.

Bill had a detailed knowledge of the world, especially of the Soviet Union through his work with the CIA. When the Soviet Union collapsed, he began to think of how he could serve the people that he'd once worked against. Bill talked with the staffs of several churches and proposed a plan to go into Minsk, Belarus, taking humanitarian aid and Bibles. With his

"Part of discovering our purpose involves reflecting on what we've gone through, and then reaching out to others going through similar struggles."

knowledge of the Soviet Union, his unique ability to deal with people and his ability to move massive amounts of supplies across the world, he knew he could make a difference.

Bill's strategy was simple: Discover the needs and seek to meet them with the love of Jesus. Within seven years, the organization he founded:

- Sent more than one million Bibles to Belarus;

WEEK FIVE

- Delivered 1.8 million dollars of medical supplies yearly;
- Distributed more than sixteen tons of food;
- Distributed thousands of dollars for clothing;
- Distributed hundreds of library book sets, which were given to churches, schools, hospitals, prisons, youth camps and public offices.

Bill and a team of local ministers also trained hundreds of prison chaplains to work with prisoners and helped the effort to start crisis pregnancy centers in Minsk. As Bill's vision became a reality, he literally changed an entire country of ten million people by meeting needs at every level of society. Thousands have come to know Jesus' love and grace through his work.

We're not all called to this magnitude of impact, but we can discover our purpose by exploring how our background connects with our gifts. I know one successful businessman who often traveled to Mexico for work. As he traveled, he asked God how his experience could help the people there. Now he sends more than 1,500 Christmas gifts a year to needy children in Mexico. Each gift includes a Spanish Bible and plenty of candy. The joy of sharing God's Word with children in remote areas brings him more blessings than he gives.

A woman overcame colon cancer and uses the experience to share her faith with other cancer survivors. "Who would have thought my cancer would bring someone to Christ?" she asks. God did.

God can take all that we've been through and use it to make an incredible impact for Him. Experience is not only a great teacher; it's a powerful equipper in developing our gifts.

POINT TO PONDER

God wants to use your family, educational and vocational backgrounds for a greater purpose.

VERSE TO REMEMBER

"God doesn't want us to be shy with his gifts, but bold and loving and sensible." 2 Timothy 1:7 (MSG)

QUESTION TO CONSIDER

What family, educational or vocational experiences have you had that you can use to help others today?

WEEK FIVE

NOTES

UNLIKELY JOURNEY

He grew up Jewish and traveled between parents who lived in two different states. It wasn't ideal, but he managed. Through high school he bounced back and forth between parents and cities every few years. He attended college in Las Vegas and then settled there. Soon after, he met and married a wonderful woman and they had two children.

"...from everyone who has been given much, much will be demanded; and from the one who has been entrusted with much, much more will be asked."
Luke 12:48b (NIV)

One day a friend from work invited them to church. They liked it and began attending regularly. It seemed like a good thing to do and

had a positive affect on their whole family. They liked the messages and always walked away with something to think about. And that was that.

Nine years later big things were happening at work. Incredible opportunities brought intense demands and increasing levels of stress. In the midst of it all, God began tugging at him. He tried to fill the void he felt with a whirlwind of activities and the busyness of work, family and too many commitments.

Just before departing on a three-week business trip, he came to church and heard a message on stress. It was a divine appointment! The message spoke directly to him, emphasizing that Christ doesn't want us to carry our burdens alone. Taking the burden off his shoulders was an entirely new concept. God had been planting seeds and they were beginning to take root.

"He tried to fill the void he felt with a whirlwind of activities and the busyness of work, family and too many commitments."

The trip's agenda was a hectic three weeks of meetings and multiple presentations per meeting. Public speaking was not his forte and the future of his corporation and millions of dollars were at stake. Then, remembering what he heard at church, he decided to pray before each meeting. He asked Christ to relieve the anxiety and remove the stress. He asked God to help him speak freely and clearly without obvious fear. It worked. The meetings were a success.

He'd always attributed things that went well to being in the right place at the right time or being good at what he did. But slowly he realized that God had played a large part in his life. Things began to make sense in a brand new way. During his time away, he began to feel God calling him. He wanted to reorient and dedicate his life to Christ.

After returning home he decided to tell the pastor how the message on stress he'd heard at church had impacted him. During that meeting, he gave his life to Christ and accepted Him as his Lord and Savior. And that was just the beginning. God had kingdom-building plans for him and slowly they began to unfold.

He strongly felt God wanting him to serve, so he prayed and listened. He didn't know what God wanted him to do; he just wanted to serve and obey. He wanted to give back to God, but didn't yet know how or where. In the meantime, he listened faithfully through prayer and studying his Bible. He was thirsty for God's truth and for seeking God's will in his life. He leaned on the latter part of the verse in Luke 12:48 (NIV), "...from everyone who has been given much, much will be demanded; and from the one who has been entrusted with much, much more will be asked."

He was baptized, started taking classes at church, took a spiritual gift assessment and joined a small group Bible study. God had changed his life, but he felt something else was unfolding. A pastor spent time faithfully mentoring him and together they prayed God would reveal how he could serve and give back to God. He wanted to live the verses shared in Philippians 2: 5-7 (NLT): "Your attitude should be the same that Christ Jesus had. Though he was God, he did not demand and cling to his rights as God. He made himself nothing; he took the humble position of

WEEK FIVE

a slave and appeared in human form."

He prayed Psalm 139:23-24 (NASB): "Search me, O God, and know my heart; Try me and know my anxious thoughts; and see if there be any hurtful way in me, And lead me in the everlasting way." And God did. When a pastor suggested a place to serve he knew in his heart it was right for him.

He'd learned what his gifts were, but it all came together when he started serving. And God has blessed that step of faith. Using his gifts of giving, discernment, administration and leadership have brought him great joy and filled a need in the church. God opened up an opportunity for him to serve full-time and he obeyed.

His identity is in Christ, his relationship with Christ is secure and he thinks more about helping others than what is in it for himself. The urge to constantly be engaged in a whirlwind of activities has ceased. Today he prefers to serve quietly and humbly, often with a shy demeanor and a wry smile that shows a glimpse of the joy he experiences inside. He serves God by serving others, and through his gifts he blesses.

POINT TO PONDER

God has kingdom-building plans for you. Pray, listen and trust in Him to reveal how you can best serve Him.

VERSE TO REMEMBER

"...from everyone who has been given much, much will be demanded; and from the one who has been entrusted with much, much more will be asked." Luke 12:48b (NIV)

QUESTIONS TO CONSIDER

Have you taken the time to pray, listen and trust God to reveal how He can use you? In the meantime, where are you serving Him today?

WEEK FIVE

NOTES

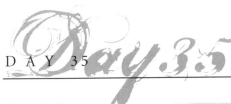

FAN
INTO
FLAME

Have you ever noticed how simultaneously diverse and alike students can be? No matter where they live, kids seem to reflect certain commonalities.

I'm struck by the similarities of nonconformists. No matter where I travel, there's always a group of students whose banner is to be independent of influence and to rage against the status quo. They're on a quest

> *"...I remind you to fan into flame the gift of God..."*
> 2 Timothy 1:6b (NIV)

to express their individuality. And while I admire their passion, I find it ironic that they travel in herds of like-minded, identically dressed, nonconforming conformists.

WEEK FIVE

Perhaps the most consistent similarity is their response to the question of entertainment. I've talked to students in small towns and big cities, from the Midwest to the northeast, to the southwest. Yet it seems that in no pocket of our country, in any town or city, no matter the size, topography or any local wonder of man or nature, is there anything in any form for kids to do. In asking the question, "What is there to do in your town?" I always receive the same lament. The universal response is an emphatic, "NOTHING!" Almost every kid in junior high or high school will say there's nothing to do in his or her town.

You know, they may be on to something we, as adults, tend to overlook. Because life affords us certain freedoms and resources, we forget a lesson once learned in our youth. No matter what the expanse of our resources, we inevitably run out of ways to entertain ourselves.

I marvel at the wealth and lifestyles in our world. Yet, even the rich and famous run out of ways to entertain themselves. Have you ever watched *MTV Cribs, It'$ Good to Be*, or the grandfather of them all, *Lifestyles of the Rich and Famous*? It's easy to fall into the trap of envy looking at the decadence and lifestyles of those we celebrate. But it doesn't matter who you are, where you go or how much you've acquired. Running after self-gratification results in train-wrecking your life. Self-gratification has a low ceiling because self-centeredness is not what we were created for.

Though we may run out of ways to entertain ourselves, we'll never run out of ways to serve others. The good news is, serving others brings us greater joy and is ultimately more fulfilling and gratifying than entertaining ourselves. Serving others is part of the design for which we were created. Ephesians 2:10a (NIV) is one of the verses we've continually come back to in this study. It says, "...we are God's workmanship, created in Christ Jesus to do good works." In 2 Timothy 1:6, Paul tells Timothy to "**fan into flame** the gift of God." These two passages encourage us to learn more about how God has gifted us and to find ways to continuously put our gifts to use. Although serving others may run against our human nature, it's securely a part of God's nature. He has spiritually gifted you with ways to serve, and yes, even the desire to do so. It's in you somewhere! Using your spiritual gifts is all about serving others. Maybe that's why the Bible so strongly encourages us to discover our gifts and find ways to use them.

"Self-gratification has a low ceiling because self-centeredness is not what we were created for."

In Timothy's case, the flame of passion in the use of his gift had apparently begun to flicker. Paul's words indicate that timidity, pressure and insecurity may have been cause for Timothy's much needed encouragement. These reasons can be included in my own long list of needing encouragement to "fan the flame" of the gift God's given me. I need reminders to keep looking for new ways to put my gift to use or I revert to a natural bent toward self-indulgent comfort quests. Galatians 6:9 (NIV) says, "Let us not become weary in doing good, for at the proper time we will reap a harvest if we do not give up."

Using the gifts God has given you is rewarding, but difficult too. It's easy to neglect them. That's why it is so important to keep learning and

WEEK FIVE

developing your experiences so you can better serve God. In a world filled with so many people, with so many problems and hardships, there are endless opportunities to share your gifts. It's one of the best ways to experience what 2 Peter 1:4 (NIV) describes as "participation in the divine nature."

POINT TO PONDER

You'll always run out of ways to entertain yourself, but never ways to serve others.

VERSE TO REMEMBER

"...I remind you to fan into flame the gift of God..."
2 Timothy 1:6b (NIV)

QUESTIONS TO CONSIDER

Where are you spending your time and efforts? Are you chasing self-gratification or using your gifts to serve others?

NOTES

Day 35

EXPERIENCING THE JOY OF SERVING

"Jesus looked at them and said,
'With man this is impossible, but
with God all things are possible.'"

Matthew 19:26 (NIV)

PASSIVE OR PASSIONATE?

You're on your way to living with passion. You can choose to embrace this journey *passionately* or go along *passively*. It's totally up to you. But God desires a life of passion for you. He's actively working to bring people, places and events into your journey to move you toward living out the passion of His heart for you.

"I welcome the chance to take my share in the church's part of that suffering. When I became a servant in this church, I experienced this suffering as a sheer gift, God's way of helping me serve you, laying out the whole truth."

Colossians 1:24b-25 (MSG)

WEEK SIX

In his book, *The Journey of Desire,* John Eldridge says, "The One who created you and set all those loves and gifts in your heart, the One who has shaped all your life experiences (including the ones that seem to make no sense), this God has prepared a place for you that is more than a perfect fit for all your gifts and quirks and personality traits—even those you don't know you have."

The first key to passionate living is to start where you are right now. Where are you living? What are you doing for a living? What are your trials? Surrender it all and be prepared to see your eyes open to the incredible journey He's already taking you on.

Nicholas Herman lived in the 1600's. He fought for the French army during the Thirty Years War. After the war, he worked for an official in the French Treasury. Desiring a richer, deeper spiritual life he then joined a Carmelite monastery in Paris at the age of fifty. With all his experience, he imagined God would use him greatly. His assignment? The kitchen. He was insulted and grudgingly carried out his chores.

One day Nicholas decided to change his attitude. He began to realize that even the most menial tasks were holy when done for God's glory. Christ lived in him, so wherever he was, the Lord was there too. Nicholas' countenance began to change. Leaders noticed and began seeking him out to discover the key to his radiance. His conversations with others were eventually published in a book called *The Practice of the Presence of God,* attributed to Brother Lawrence-Nicholas' monastery name.

Where has God placed you? Surrender to Him and watch your passion and love for Him transform you. Psalm 18:20-24 (MSG) says, "God made my life complete when I placed all the pieces before him. When

I got my act together, he gave me a fresh start. Now I'm alert to God's ways; I don't take God for granted. Every day I review the ways he works; I feel put back together, and I'm watching my step. God rewrote the text of my life when I opened the book of my heart to his eyes."

The second key to passionate living is waiting on His timing and trusting His sovereignty. God will put doors before you. Be careful of either ignoring a door or forcing entry. Living a passionate life involves waiting to see which doors He opens and which He closes. Focus your attention on what *He* is doing, not on what *you* are doing.

In *When The Heart Waits*, author Sue Monk Kidd says, "We posture ourselves in ways that allow God to heal, transform, and create us." God's Word assures us, "The steps of good men are directed by the Lord. He directs each step they take. If they fall it isn't fatal, for the Lord holds them with His hand"(Psalm 37:23-24, LB).

> "You can choose to embrace this journey *passionately* or go along *passively*."

The third key is recognizing suffering as part of passionate living. I knew at an early age God gave me the desire to be a counselor. But I had no idea He'd take me on a journey to empathize with people's pain and suffering. I married right out of college. We planned for my husband to look for a job in the city where I wanted to attend graduate school. But God had other plans. Instead of pursuing my dream I found myself trying to figure out what I would do. Why wasn't God allowing me to work toward my calling? When I finally found a job, I worked for only a

WEEK SIX

few weeks before learning I needed major surgery. The doctors said if I planned on having children, I'd better do it now!

My life was completely redirected. It wasn't until my early thirties, after experiencing much brokenness and loss that God reopened a door allowing me to become a counselor. But He wasn't through teaching me about utter and complete dependence on Him. As I learned the skills to help marriages survive, mine crumbled. No matter what I tried, it wasn't enough. God was wrestling the "me" out of myself and it was painful. I walked away with the limp of a failed marriage and now lived the irony of being a divorced Christian marriage and family therapist. God's purpose was larger than mine. He took my sins and those of others in my life and now uses them to bring healing to others. Through it all, I've found no greater joy than seeing my hurts and brokenness used by God to heal someone else.

In *The Significance of Jesus*, Brennan Manning says, "When we have hit bottom and are emptied of all we thought important to us, then we truly pray, truly become humble and detached, and live in the bright darkness of faith. In the midst of the emptying we know that God has not deserted us. He has merely removed the obstacles keeping us from a deeper union with him." At this point you truly learn to live with passion, completely surrendered to His way, His timing and rest in His sovereignty.

POINT TO PONDER

The keys to living a life of passion are surrender, waiting, resting and suffering.

VERSE TO REMEMBER

"I welcome the chance to take my share in the church's part of that suffering. When I became a servant in this church, I experienced this suffering as a sheer gift, God's way of helping me serve you, laying out the whole truth." Colossians 1:24-25 (MSG)

QUESTION TO CONSIDER

How might your current circumstance be a call to live more passionately?

WEEK SIX

NOTES

THE BOSS

Do it all for His glory. We all have the same job and the same boss. Our job is to serve our Lord, our Master, our boss. Keeping this in perspective leads not only to job enrichment and satisfaction, it leads to *life* enrichment and satisfaction. Does that mean we all do the same thing? Absolutely not! God uniquely made each of us in His image. We all have different spiritual gifts, a unique personality and diverse life experiences to draw upon. So how can we all have the same job?

"Whatever you do, work at it with all your heart, as working for the Lord, not for men, since you know that you will receive an inheritance from the Lord as a reward. It is the Lord Christ you are serving."

Colossians 3:23-24 (NIV)

Keeping Jesus as your focal point and modeling your life and actions after Him will free you of worldly measurements that lead to dissatisfaction. Comparing yourself to others, be it in job title, rank, intelligence, wealth, material accumulation, beauty, status, popularity, etc., only brings disappointment and frustration. Releasing yourself from such concerns gives you the freedom to use your God-given talents and serve Him.

Before I accepted Christ as my personal Lord and Savior, I often had days at work when I felt like quitting! I didn't always like what I did and I didn't care for my boss. Accepting Christ didn't erase those frustrations but it was the beginning of the end! Establishing a relationship with Him and understanding my purpose in life led to the end of those frustrations. Now when I'm working I know why I'm here and who my boss is. I no longer have the desire to quit.

"Keeping Jesus as your focal point and modeling your life and actions after Him will free you of worldly measurements that lead to dissatisfaction."

God can use you right now, just as you are. When you focus on Him, you serve Him by modeling a Christ-like character in what you do, how you interact with people and how you process and make decisions. Sometimes the most effective way to share your faith is the way you carry yourself at home, in the workplace or wherever you are.

We live in a world that says there are no moral absolutes. Character is often based on convenience or circumstances. But when you live out a Christ-like character people will notice. They'll ask why you behave the way you do. All Christ-followers can practice this kind of evangelism.

Colossians 3:23a (NIV) says, "Whatever you do, work at it with all your heart, as if working for the Lord..." This verse is often used to help people understand that all jobs and vocations can be used for God's glory. Although this is extremely important, the verse doesn't say whenever you work, but whatever you do. That means work, chores, parenting, schoolwork or having fun. It means when you're with others or alone. Whatever you do, do it all for God's glory!

Recently I celebrated with some church volunteers at a dinner when a woman commented about looking forward to retiring. "You'll never retire," I replied. She was somewhat taken aback by this comment until I continued. "Oh, you may retire from your job, but you'll never quit working for the Lord!" She smiled in agreement. We'll continue to work for Him as long as we are here on earth. Why not do so in everything you do, with all your heart as a shining light for Christ?

WEEK SIX

POINT TO PONDER

Do it all for His glory.

VERSE TO REMEMBER

"Whatever you do, work at it with all your heart, as working for the Lord, not for men." Colossians 3:23 (NIV)

QUESTIONS TO CONSIDER

What's keeping you from serving the Lord in everything you do? What barriers exist? What steps can you take to remove those barriers and keep Christ as the focus of all you do?

NOTES

I SURRENDER

Jesus' method of ministry, the thing that made Him so effective, was his self-denial—surrendering everything to live (and die) for God and others. Had He not died on a cross, you'd likely never have heard of Him. And that's God's call to you—to surrender everything, take up your cross and follow Christ. Taking up your cross is not a call to sacrifice, to

> *"Jesus looked at them and said, 'With man this is impossible, but with God all things are possible.'"*
>
> Matthew 19:26 (NIV)

tithe, to volunteer, to live with a husband with bad breath or to go on a mission—it's a call to die to yourself and live for Christ. God can do great and eternally significant things through a life fully surrendered to Him:

"For whoever exalts himself will be humbled, but whoever humbles himself will be exalted" (Matthew 23:12, NIV). But does it work? Do you believe that putting yourself last, abandoning everything and surrendering to God will make an impact? Ask Aggie Hurst. Jim Cymbala shares her story in his book, *Fresh Power*.

In 1921, a missionary couple named David and Svea Flood went with their two-year-old son from Sweden to what was then called the Belgian Congo in the heart of Africa. At the village of N'dolera, the chief refused their entry. So, the Floods went a half-mile up the slope to build their mud hut. They prayed for a spiritual breakthrough, but received none. Their only contact with any of the villagers was with one young boy who was allowed to sell them chickens and eggs twice a week. Svea decided if he was the only African she could talk to, she'd try leading the boy to Jesus. Over time she succeeded.

But there were no other encouragements. Then Svea became pregnant. This was a frightening thing in the middle of a primitive wilderness. When the time came for her to give birth, the village chief softened enough to allow a midwife to assist her. A little girl was born, whom they named Aina. But the delivery was exhausting and Svea was already weak from bouts of malaria. The young mother died 17 days later.

In that moment, something inside David Flood snapped. He dug a crude grave, buried his twenty-seven-year-old wife and took his children back down the mountain to the mission station. Giving his newborn daughter to another missionary couple, he snarled, "I'm going back to Sweden. I've lost my wife, and I obviously can't take care of the baby. God has ruined my life." With that he left, rejecting his calling and God Himself.

WEEK SIX

The baby was given to some American missionaries, who changed her name to Aggie and brought her to the United States at the age of three. Cymbala goes on to tell how she grew up in America, married and moved to Seattle where her husband became president of a Christian college. One day a religious magazine appeared in her mailbox. She had no idea who sent it, but as she turned the pages a photo stopped her cold. There in a primitive setting was a grave with a white cross bearing the name SVEA FLOOD.

The magazine article told the story of missionaries who'd come to N'dolera long ago, the birth of a white baby, the death of a young mother and one little African boy who was led to Christ. The article continued with what happened next. All the whites left the area. But the boy grew up and persuaded the chief to let him build a school in the village. Gradually he won all his students to Christ. The children led their parents to Christ. Even the chief became a Christian. Today there were six hundred believers in that one village.

Aggie decided to search for her biological father. Now an old man, David Flood had remarried, fathered four more children and generally wasted his life on alcohol. Still bitter, he had one rule in his family: "Never mention the name of God—because God took everything from me."

Aggie found her father lying in a rumpled bed in a small, dirty apartment littered with liquor bottles. When he saw her, he began to cry, "Aina, I never meant to give you away." Taking him in her arms she replied, "It's all right, Papa, God took care of me." The man instantly tensed and the tears stopped. "God forgot all of us. Our lives have been ruined because of Him," he barked, turning his face to the wall.

Undaunted, Aggie continued, "Papa, I have a story to tell you. You didn't go to Africa in vain. Mama didn't die in vain. The little boy you won to the Lord grew up to win the whole village to Jesus Christ. Today there are six hundred African people serving the Lord. Papa, Jesus loves you. He's never hated you." The old man turned and looked into his daughter's eyes. His body relaxed. By the end of that afternoon, he returned to the God he had resented for so long.

Cymbala then shares how a few years later Aggie and her husband were attending an evangelism conference in England, when a report was given from Zaire (the former Belgian Congo). The superintendent of the national church, representing some 110,000 baptized believers, spoke enthusiastically of the Gospel's spread in his nation. Afterward, Aggie went up and asked the man if he'd ever heard of David and Svea Flood. "It was Svea who led me to Jesus Christ," he replied. "I was the boy who brought food to your parents before you were born." (From, *Fresh Power*, by Jim Cymbala and Dean Merrill.)

> "God can do great and eternally significant things through a life fully surrendered to Him."

This remarkable growth in the kingdom of God all stemmed from David and Svea Flood's sacrificial surrender to God, allowing the Holy Spirit to work through them. Some might say, "What a tragedy to lose a young wife and mother." But I think Svea Flood would say, "What an incredible privilege—giving my life to win a nation to Christ." Self-denial and sur-

WEEK SIX

render to God is explosive. Do you believe it?

POINT TO PONDER

God can do great and eternally significant things through a life surrendered to Him.

VERSE TO REMEMBER

"Jesus looked at them and said, 'With man this is impossible, but with God all things are possible.'" Matthew 19:26 (NIV)

QUESTION TO CONSIDER

When you come to Christ, He demands that you surrender everything— what are you still holding on to?

NOTES

A SHAPE TO ADMIRE

We've all envied another person's gifts. It's human nature to want what we don't have. And so we think, "I wish I could sing like him. Motherhood comes so naturally to her. If only I were an articulate speaker like she is. I wish I had the business experience he does. Why can't I be more creative like her?" But if we surrender to these types of feelings, we

> "Yet, O Lord, you are our Father. We are the clay, you are the potter; we are all the work of your hand."
>
> Isaiah 64:8 (NIV)

start doubting the gifts God gave us and even question the way He created us to be. Eventually, our gifts may seem unimportant and sadly, we may stop using them altogether. This is not part of God's design for us!

Throughout the Bible, God is referred to as the Potter, and we, as His clay. Would a potter intentionally create something ugly or worthless to him? No. He creates only what is beautiful and serves His purpose. Isaiah 64:8 (NIV) says, "Yet, O Lord, you are our Father. We are the clay, you are the potter; we are all the work of your hand." God has the same right over us as a potter has over his clay. A potter has a design in mind before crafting a new piece. Bearing down on the clay with his hands, he gently shapes it into the desired form. Each work of art the potter creates has different characteristics and distinct qualities that separate it from the rest. Likewise, when we were created by the Father's hand, He shaped each of us into His desired form, each taking on our own beautiful, unique shape—a shape to admire.

God crafted each of us in His own hands. Using precision and forethought He made each of us to be exactly who He wanted us to be. Knowing that, what right do we have to be dissatisfied with who He made us to be? Romans 9:20-21(NIV) says, "But who are you, O man, to talk back to God? Shall what is formed say to him who formed it, 'Why did you make me like this?' Does not the potter have the right to make out of the same lump of clay some pottery for noble purposes and some for common use?"

Whether you feel created for noble purpose or common use, remember that our all-knowing, powerful God created you. With unlimited resources and endless imagination, He could've designed you with any number of gifts. Yet He specifically chose yours for a reason. There's something unique about you! You are unlike anyone else.

God didn't give you your gifts to impress the world or to gain rec-

WEEK SIX

ognition. He wants you to develop them for His glory. Galatians 6:4-5 (MSG) says, "Make a careful exploration of who you are and the work you have been given, and then sink yourself into that. Don't be impressed with yourself. Don't compare yourself with others. Each of you must take responsibility for doing the creative best you can with your own life."

God wants you to understand the way He created you. He wants you to recognize and celebrate your gifts. Rather than comparing yourself with others and thinking either too highly or too lowly of yourself, He wants you to take responsibility and use the gifts, He's entrusted you with, to the best of your ability.

"Whether you feel created for noble purpose or common use, remember that our all-knowing, powerful God created you."

Imagine all the different gifts represented within your church. If everyone all had the same abilities, it'd be a very boring church. What if everybody was teachers or childcare workers? What if everyone was in the choir? It would be quite crowded up on those risers. Instead of giving everyone identical gifts, God created each of us with unique abilities, so when we come together as a church we benefit each other, build each other up and glorify Him!

Paul writes, "Just as our bodies have many parts and each part has a special function, so it is with Christ's body. We are all parts of his one body, and each of us has different work to do. And since we are all one body in Christ, we belong to each other, and each of us needs all the others. God has given each of us the ability to do certain things well" (Romans 12:4-6, MSG).

Let's be thankful for the abilities we've been given. Instead of comparing ourselves with others, let's rejoice in what we have, knowing God gave each of us specific gifts for a reason and it's our responsibility and privilege to develop and use them to His glory.

The next step:

- Make a list of the gifts, talents and resources you've been given.
- Take time to thank God for blessing you with uniquely designed gifts.
- If you're experiencing any insecurities or self-doubt regarding your gifts, pray that God will strengthen you and make you confident in the person He's created you to be.
- Ask God to show you ways to use your gifts for His glory, whether at church, in your home or family relationships, in the workplace—wherever!

WEEK SIX

POINT TO PONDER

God has individually shaped you and given you unique gifts.

VERSE TO REMEMBER

"Yet, O Lord, you are our Father. We are the clay, you are the potter; we are all the work of your hand." Isaiah 64:8 (NIV)

QUESTIONS TO CONSIDER

What is it about you that others may envy? How can you use this gift or ability to serve others for God's glory?

NOTES

A
LIFE
RECONSTRUCTED

It was a cold December morning when the handicap bus pulled up to the hospital in Portland, Oregon. Cheryl needed help in order to get off the bus. The hospital was a familiar place for her. For the past five years she'd worked as a registered nurse at this same hospital. She was well acquainted with the walkway to the building and the intricate maze of

"And we know that in all things God works for the good of those who love him, who have been called according to his purpose."

Romans 8:28 (NIV)

hallways inside. She'd walked this entry and through these halls hundreds of times. She'd cared for countless patients within these walls. But

this early December morning was different from all the others. On this day, Cheryl was the patient and not the nurse. As Cheryl was helped off the bus, she saw familiar coworkers walking through the front doors of the hospital. She was unable to join them.

She used to walk briskly up the pathway to the front doors but now it took effort, determination and the help of both a cane and a brace to walk even twenty feet. She used to talk with coworkers walking from the parking lot to the front doors, but now she could only utter a few simple words, unable to even string them together to form a sentence. Life had dramatically changed.

One day three months earlier, Cheryl went to work as usual. She had a nagging headache and as the day progressed she began having difficulty understanding and following what people were saying. She attributed the "mental fog" to her headache and the fatigue and stress of a long hectic day. Toward the end of her shift, things were getting noticeably worse. She was grateful to check out and head for home. By the time Cheryl got to her car the fuzziness and fog in her mind had again worsened. She decided to read a few verses from her Bible before getting on the busy freeway leading home. To her surprise, Cheryl had difficulty comprehending the words she read. She tried to read aloud but the words she spoke were different from those she read on the page. As a trained nurse, Cheryl grew concerned she might be having a stroke. She flagged down a parking lot security guard who took her back to the emergency room. When she tried to get out of his car, she discovered the right side of her body had lost all feeling. Once inside the hospital, a CT scan revealed that Cheryl had a large brain hemorrhage. Her life would never be the same.

WEEK SIX

Cheryl's loss was great and came at many levels. In the early days, she was unable to sit up or move her head without feeling nauseous. Her right side was completely paralyzed. Drool would form at the right side of her mouth and she was unable to take care of it. She lost the ability to speak and was unable to write numbers or letters. She wanted to communicate and knew what she wanted to say, but couldn't get her mouth to say the words or her hand to write the letters. After three months of in-patient physical therapy she was now returning to the hospital to begin the long and difficult process of outpatient physical, occupational and speech therapy. Losing the ability to walk and speak had shattered her dream of one day serving as a medi-

"Losing the ability to walk and speak had shattered her dream of one day serving as a medical missionary."

cal missionary. And if all that weren't enough, Cheryl would also face the break-up of her eight-year marriage in the months to come. All her hopes and dreams had vanished.

Cheryl had graduated from Biola University in 1975 with a nursing degree and a minor in biblical studies. She planned to one day serve God as a medical missionary to the Muslim people. Those plans now seemed like a distant dream. In her early days of rehabilitation, one Bible verse stood out in Cheryl's mind. It was Romans 8:28 (NIV) where Paul wrote, "And we know that in all things God works for the good of those who love him, who have been called according to his purpose." As she was

helped off the bus to begin a new phase of therapy, she wondered about God's plans for her life. How would God bring good from her circumstances? What did He have planned for her life?

If you fast-forward Cheryl's story to today, it's easy to see the good God brought to this wonderful and beautiful woman of faith. Cheryl learned firsthand that God uses our pain and struggles to help us minister to others and to bring glory to Himself. Traces of her stroke are still evident in Cheryl's speech and step, but her efforts in therapy and at the gym have paid off. She's relearned how to walk and communicate. She sees how God uses her physical limitations as strengths when she ministers to others.

Today, Cheryl uses her experiences to minister to others. She's led support groups for stroke survivors at various hospitals and she regularly visits stroke patients as a volunteer with the American Stroke Association. Five years ago she began a support group at her church for brain-injured people. Cheryl believes God has healed her enough to minister to others but that He still uses the physical effects of her stroke to allow her "to be a living demonstration that God is faithful." Cheryl expresses her compassion for Muslim people through a monthly prayer group she started six years ago. She and others gather and pray for persecuted Christians around the world, including those in countries that are predominantly Muslim. Deep down Cheryl understands, in a way that most of us really can't comprehend, that "in all things, God works for the good of those who love Him."

WEEK SIX

POINT TO PONDER

God uses your painful circumstances to help you care for others dealing with similar difficulties.

VERSE TO REMEMBER

"And we know that in all things God works for the good of those who love him, who have been called according to his purpose."
Romans 8:28 (NIV)

QUESTION TO CONSIDER

What "impossible" situations have you navigated through in your life? In what ways can God turn your experiences into ways to serve others for Him?

NOTES

APPENDIX

Abbreviations and Translations Used

CEV: Contemporary English Version
New York: American Bible Society (1995)

GN: Good News (also called Today's English Version)
New York: American Bible Society (1992)

KJV: King James Version

LB: Living Bible
Wheaton, IL: Tyndale House Publishers (1979)

MSG: The Message
Colorado Springs: Navpress (1993)

NASB: New American Standard Bible
Anaheim, CA: Foundation Press (1973)

NCV: New Century Version
Dallas: Word Bibles (1991)

NIV: New International Version
Colorado Springs: International Bible Society (1978, 1984)

NKJV: New King James Version
Nashville: Thomas Nelson Publishers (1982)

NLT: New Living Translation
Wheaton, IL: Tyndale House Publishers (1996)